MW01629430

GARTH BROOKS
THE ANTHOLOGY | PART FOUR

Produced by

**MELCHER
MEDIA**

124 West 13th Street
New York, NY 10011
www.melcher.com

10 9 8 7 6 5 4 3 2 1

Manufactured in China
Library of Congress Cataloging-in-Publication
Data available upon request.

Standard Edition: 978-1-59591-140-7
Limited Edition: 978-1-59591-141-4

GARTH BROOKS
THE ANTHOLOGY | PART FOUR

GOING HOME

WRITTEN BY

GARTH BROOKS

WITH WARREN ZANES

MELCHER MEDIA

PEARL RECORDS

TABLE OF CONTENTS

FOREWORD

Working on this *Anthology* series has been one of the great joys of my life. I can't tell you that I knew what I was getting into when the project started, but I look back and feel lucky that I was one of the people involved. It's been an extraordinary process, going deep with Garth, his songwriters, his studio and management teams, the musicians who have worked with him, his friends, and, of course, Trisha Yearwood. I've learned a lot and laughed a lot along the way. We have a few more volumes to go, but I'm already worried about what I'm going to do with myself when it's over.

Now, you're not supposed to have a favorite among your children, and you're not supposed to have a favorite book in a series you're working on. But, between us, this installment in the *Anthology* series, Volume IV, is special to me. I've come to know more about Garth as we've worked on each book, but never did I learn as much about him as I did with this one. Maybe it's because I'm a parent myself; maybe it's because I've gone through divorce and came out the other side. I don't know.

THIS IS A STORY UNLIKE **ANY I'VE EVER HEARD.**

What I do know is that this book has a story unlike any I've ever heard. The short version you probably know already: One of the most successful and beloved artists in the history of popular music had a big party celebrating 100 million in sales, a milestone few will achieve, and then, on that same day, announced his retirement. And that artist, still young, walked away from it all. This is the stuff that happens in movies, not in Nashville, or Los Angeles, or New York, or London, or, if you want to know the truth, Scranton or Boise. So, why'd he do it? That's really what this book is about: why he did it, and how he did it. And that's the part that stirred something in me.

When your dreams come true and you get to do that thing you always thought about as a kid, you have to honor that. Go live it, fully and completely. And when you have your own kids, be there for them, love them, fully and completely. But sometimes it happens that those two things occur at the same time, and really, who wants to let go of either of them, your dreams or your kids? So, most folks try to find some middle position—work a little less, stop by the toy store more frequently, try to find a balance. When it comes to the life of the touring musician, however, it's not easy to find a middle position. There just aren't enough toy stores. And when a parent has to go on the road, that means they're gone. When it comes to family life, the musician's line of work can be pretty unforgiving.

When Garth came to that crossroads, he did something he felt he had to do: He retired from touring and recording new albums, no matter the demand for his music or the dreams he could still realize. Then he took the other full-time gig, fatherhood, on the kids' terms. There was going to be some training involved. His supervisors were three young girls. And the beginning of that new position overlapped with the end of his first marriage, which gave Garth one more reason to be an at-home dad. Kids can come through divorce okay, but they do a lot better if their parents go through it with them, not phoning it in from the local tavern or the back of a tour bus. Sounds simple, right? It isn't. Not in my experience.

So, Garth held that press conference, letting the public know he was retiring. It caught a lot of people by surprise. But the truth was that this decision had been in Garth's mind for years. In talking with Garth's longtime producer Allen Reynolds, Allen said this to me: "Since Taylor was born, the first child, Garth's told me, 'Look, when my kids can't travel, I'm off the road, 'cause I'm going to be there for them like my parents were there for me.' And I respected that. So, yeah, it was an

KIDS DO A LOT BETTER WITH DIVORCE **IF THEIR PARENTS GO THROUGH IT WITH THEM.**

idea that had been around for some time." Of course, a lot of people declare such things without following through, in part because it's the work that keeps a household going. In Garth's case, though, here was an artist celebrating 100 million in sales. There would be financial stability for some time to come. So, he left a career he loved deeply because there was something he loved more. For me, as a single dad who had grown up with music as my favorite place to be, this story got me right in the chest.

In my mind, the symbol at the heart of this book is the little yellow house in Oklahoma. Soon after the 100 million party, Garth moved into it with his three daughters. As I did interviews for this book, I kept hearing about it, how small it was, how full of life it was, about the kids' drawings all over the kitchen. I had to go see it for myself to understand—and no one had exaggerated! It's tiny. And it wasn't some temporary situation—they lived in it for five years. In time, Trisha Yearwood would join them, forming a family.

So, this is a story about choices, about leaving things you love because there's something you love more, something that needs you. Garth moved from Nashville in part because you couldn't retire from active work in country music and stay in Nashville. So, there he was, in Oklahoma, the biggest changes of his life in front of him, not knowing exactly what he was doing, trusting his heart, his instinct, God, and his teachers, those girls. To me, it's an adventure story. But most adventures are about leaving home, and this one is about finding it.

—Warren Zanes

L to R: Dewayne Blackwell, Larry Bastian, Kim Williams, Stephanie Davis, Garth, Tony Arata, Victoria Shaw, Kent Blazy, and Pat Alger

THE GREAT IN-BETWEEN

G: The 100 million party came at the end of 2000. It had been just over a decade since we'd put out the first album. You talk about dreams coming true? But there I was celebrating all of that success, surrounded by the people who made it possible, and inside of me I knew that all I wanted right then, after all those years of looking to stand out…was to be somebody who blended in, because this is now about the kids.

STORME WARREN: The 100 million milestone was this incredible event at the Bridgestone Arena. I produced a thirty-minute video of his ten-year career for that. It was one of the coolest projects I had ever worked on. We had about seventy-two hours to put it together. A truck pulled up, dumped all these tapes at the front door of our production company, and we lined the hallway with his career. It really offered me a unique perspective. We saw it all, literally. Every single event and milestone of his career. And when you see all of it packed into thirty minutes, you could see why a guy would feel like he did. You go, "What else does this guy need to do?"

KAREN BYRD: At Capitol, we worked for months to bring that 100 million celebration to fruition: choosing the invitations, making the guest list, selecting the floral arrangements,

L to R: Trisha Yearwood, Martina McBride, and Steve Wariner

I'M NOT SURE ANYONE WAS READY FOR IT… **I WASN'T.**

—Bob Doyle

doing food tastings, getting the displays for each of his albums ready, coordinating the media. I was four months pregnant, so I remember the event day as very draining, but with a lot of adrenaline, just seeing everything come together. The news crew, the red carpet. Everything was so smooth. And at the party, Garth gave so much attention to songwriters. It was very emotional, and it was meaningful just to be part of that event, such a significant day. But before the party, Garth did a press conference.

BOB DOYLE: I'm not sure anyone was ready for it. I wasn't. There was no way to be ready, even if you were one of the few who knew what was coming.

STORME WARREN: I walked into that press conference not knowing. Then the rumors started swirling. But when he finally made his very emotional statement, "I'm here to announce my retirement," the words echoed in my head. It was a big deal, and it was stirring, and we all sat there and went, "He just announced his retirement after ten years on top, ten years of being the biggest superstar on the planet."

KAREN BYRD: The press conference happened at about ten o'clock in the morning. I assumed we would just be talking about marking the 100 million milestone. I don't think that anybody was expecting the retirement announcement. I organized the press conference, and I wasn't expecting what came.

STORME WARREN: I was thinking, if he wants to take a break, he should take it. But I couldn't see it as retirement. Not yet.

DAVE GANT: As a member of his band, I thought he'd have to go back on tour, wouldn't he? How could he walk away from that career and not ever want to do it again? But Mark Greenwood, our bass player, kept saying, "No, I don't think we're ever going back. I think he's done."

KAREN BYRD: I was just thinking, "Oh, wow, I guess this is really happening. He said it publicly, so this is obviously what's in his heart. But what's this going to look like? What is he going to want to do?" And it wasn't like I had a lot of downtime at the 100 million event to ask him about that. It was a big question mark, basically. But when he says something, that's what he means.

G: So, I announced my retirement and went to Oklahoma. That's where you're going to learn to be a dad, watch your marriage end, get as lost as you've ever been. How do you do that? Well, I sure didn't know—I had to go through it in order to find out how to do it. It was one of those things.

BRYAN KENNEDY: I don't think anyone knew what it was going to look like.

G: More than anything else at that moment, I wanted to be a good dad, just one-tenth what my own dad was. My job before that was pretty easy. "Honey, I'd love to help with the kids, but I got to go out on a tour where people are going to be screaming my name, and everyone's going to be trying to make me happy." My God, it was my work, but I couldn't blame not being a real dad on that anymore. Thanks to God and the people, we were more than financially secure, and these kids needed their own lives. They didn't ask to come into the world. I asked for them to come into this world. My family had made a lot of sacrifices so that I could pursue my dream. Now it was my turn to make a few. And as I found out, in time, it was no sacrifice at all. It was another gift. But before the gifts could come

through, I had to let some things go. I went into a kind of darkness I hadn't known before.

TRISHA YEARWOOD: There are times in life—and I mean for every one of us—when there's just no way around what's in front of you. You can only go forward, straight into and, hopefully, through it. And no one can do it for you.

G: I'd faced challenges earlier in my life, for sure, but in those cases I would always go to my mom. She was my support. And now she was gone. So, in the middle of it all, I was missing her so much. I leaned on friends, leaned on God. I told one of my best friends, Bryan Kennedy, that I felt like I was losing my basis, not sure where I was headed. He wrote me a note after that, something I kept with me, that I'd look at just as a kind of reminder. The note said something like, "Hey, man, sometimes there's nothing you can do, and you just have to go down. There are no handles. You're just going to have to ride it out. But you will come out the other side. Maybe in two months, maybe in two years, maybe ten. But you will come out the other side, eventually." I kept that note of his close.

A MAN,
HIS KIDS,
AND A
COUPLE
FRIENDS

CHAPTER ONE

WHEN WE FIRST GOT OUT TO OKLAHOMA, we stayed with Sandy's parents. These were great people, people I love. They were the only ones I really knew out there. Sandy and I were going to make one last run at our marriage. Because, c'mon, you were married with your family present and in front of God, so you keep thinking it's just got to work. Just one last go. We tried, but it was going to be the end of a marriage. The thing that wasn't going to end, of course, was the family. And what I came to learn is that the person you're separating from is the person you need as your best friend in the process of ending a marriage. It's the hardest time for that, but it's the thing your family needs the most. And Sandy did that for the situation, the girls, and for me.

THERE WAS GOING TO BE
A LOT OF LEARNING. —g

But going back there? It was just, well, it was dark. Nights were lonely. Not because of the place or the people. It was dark because you felt inadequate in everything that you did. You weren't a good enough dad. Sure as hell weren't a good enough husband, and that had showed in the results. We ended up finding a piece of land in between Claremore and Owasso. We gave it one last shot, but once we decided just go ahead and get it done and go through the divorce, that was by far the roughest time in my life. And I hope it continues to be the roughest. I hope I never have anything worse than that era, right there. That hurt.

We ended up moving a modular home onto the other side of the property, and Sandy moved in there. I remained in the small, maybe seven-hundred-square-foot bunkhouse where the foreman and the cowboys used to sleep.

When you walked in, the great room was all bunk beds. And then it had one foreman's room and another room for the foreman's children. That was it. It was tiny, and that's where we'd live for the next five years. The little yellow house.

Sandy and I started exchanging the kids every day at six. For fourteen years we exchanged the kids every day at six, because we didn't think it was fair that they would have to live without their mom or their dad. So, there I was, back in Oklahoma where I was raised, settled in and just getting ready for… I didn't know what. I was going to start learning every other day at 6 p.m. And there was going to be a lot of learning.

But the first hard truth I faced was this: The kids just really wanted to be with their mom, because that's all they knew. Dad didn't

understand a lot about tender stuff. I was raised with boys. I feel
so sorry for my mom and my sister, because they had to live in
a male world. It was my dad and five boys. So being around girls
was a little different for me.

When I didn't have the girls, though, I was facing a kind of
aloneness you couldn't know if you were on a bus with a bunch
of musicians and crew. It was an abrupt change I was looking at.
Maybe too abrupt? I don't know. I was always kind of an all-or-
nothing type. But there was my brother Jerry and a couple of
guys from the crew who were a part of that first year out there:
Emmett Gilliam and Ted Larkin. They helped me get to know the
ranch, set up a life out there. Emmett was from Oklahoma but
had been on the road with us since 1992. I'd known Ted Larkin
since college. I knew his family, and he knew mine. Those three
guys were a bit of a lifeline as I headed into all of this.

L to R: Emmett Gilliam, Ted Larkin, and Garth

* * *

TED LARKIN: In 1981, I was a freshman wrestler at Oklahoma State University and living in the athletic dorm. One of the first days I was there, my roommate and I had set up my stereo, which was very loud. We heard someone else's music coming from down the hall, and my roommate said, "Your stereo's louder than that." I put on some Nitty Gritty

MY DOOR FLEW OPEN, AND THERE'S A BUNCH OF GUYS STANDING THERE WITH BANJOS AND GUITARS.

—Ted Larkin

Dirty Band or something, and we cranked it up. The next thing I knew, my door flew open, and there's a bunch of guys standing there with banjos and guitars. That was my first introduction to Garth Brooks.

G: Ted is one of my oldest friends. He was living down the hall when I was rooming with my brother Kelly. Music brought us together. I taught Ted what I knew on guitar. And I always hoped that if anything happened for me that he'd come along. By the time something was happening, though, he was in the Air Force. When he was out of the Air Force, around '94–'95, he came on as a rigger. And we took that ride together. When I retired, well, we took that ride together, too.

TED LARKIN: I went from getting out of Oklahoma and really having a future and seeing the world to just a…complete stop. To go at that speed, to be engaged and seeing the world, and then it just grinds to a halt, and you have no clue what's going to happen tomorrow? That's a tough space.

G: Ted's from Oklahoma, so it made sense that he'd come to visit when I landed there with Sandy and the kids. He must've been visiting family or something. But he came by to see me and just, you know, stayed.

Ted Larkin

TED LARKIN: I'm not sure Garth knows this, and I'm not sure Trisha knows this, but they'll find out now. She was probably the biggest influence on me going to Oklahoma. I had several phone calls, talked to people who told me that Garth was having kind of a tough time. I knew it was going to be a really hard transition. Then Trisha was out in Los Angeles shooting *JAG*, the television show, and she invited me on set. So, I went over to visit and had dinner with Trisha and her parents. That night she shared with me, said, "I think he's really struggling. You really, really need to go see him. Please go see him." That's when and why I went out there to Oklahoma.

TRISHA YEARWOOD: People think being on the road is a challenge, and they're right. But it's not as hard as coming off the road. Garth had a decade of some of the busiest, steadiest work in music history. And then it all came to a stop so suddenly. Put that together with family changes and the pressure he was putting on himself to be the best dad he could be? Of course I was worried about him. But I knew he had close friends, and I knew he was going to need some of them.

G: It helped me having Ted come and stay. Like, here's someone who knows you, really knows you, from before you were Garth Brooks and, now, after. The shared history made a difference right then. And Emmett, well, Emmett was out on the road with us. He was a truck driver for years and then had to quit driving, which is when I asked him to be a stage manager. When the touring was over, he went to Oklahoma with me because he was originally from Tulsa.

Emmett Gilliam and Trisha Yearwood

IT HAD TO BE
THE HARDEST TIME
IN HIS LIFE.

—Bryan Kennedy

TRISHA YEARWOOD: Knowing his brother, along with Emmett and Ted, were there gave me a little peace. But I knew the lifestyle Garth was leaving behind. And moving to Oklahoma was just the beginning of the changes he was facing.

TED LARKIN: I'll tell you something. As much as I thought I was going to Oklahoma to be there for Garth and help him out, I was as lost as he was, if not more. I needed our friendship. I was in one of the hardest years of my life. As we were talking, I think he saw that

BRYAN KENNEDY: I don't know how he did it. He did all those things in life that you're not supposed to do at the same time: move, quit your job, get divorced. It had to be the hardest time in his life. I could see it. I could feel it.

TED LARKIN: It was a small, rundown cowboy house. When I was still in L.A., I remember my dad, who'd known Garth for years and had just visited him, saying, "What the hell am I supposed to do? He wants to live in this little cowboy house." I'm like, "Well, he can't do that, he needs more space." But, yes, he can do that. And he will. They remodeled that thing and fixed it up to where it was livable.

G: It was yellow on the outside, but everything was blue on the inside. Everything. Blue carpet, blue couches, blue tiles, blue glasses, blue handles on the silverware. I was in the one bedroom, and the girls were in the other,

EVERYTHING WAS BLUE…
EVERYTHING. —g

I was pretty lost and not sure where I needed to be, so he made the offer then. *Come stay.* My landing in Oklahoma was, well, surprising in some ways. We're going to live in this little yellow house?

and Ted was living with us, so we made a spot for him in the living room. And it was kind of bright in there. So, me and him bought a sewing machine and just made some curtains ourselves. Blue curtains.

TED LARKIN: I think there were a lot of people that were a little upset with Garth getting off the road, who just didn't understand it. But when you're around him enough, you realize that the guy does not do anything at 50 percent or even 75 percent. He's either all in or he's not going to do it. With the kids, I think that's what it was. The amount of time he spent with them and that kind of a commitment he made, that's what the whole move, the retirement, was about.

BRYAN KENNEDY: I saw the heaviness he felt. People who had been busting their butts for Garth for that whole ten or twelve years… now he's got to let them go. These people are like brothers and sisters to him. But he was ready to be there for his girls.

TED LARKIN: He kind of said, "It's what's best for them? I'm all in." He and Sandy developed a plan where they literally had the kids every other day. Everybody told him, "Man, you can't do that. It's not healthy, it's not good." But it was perfect for them. The kids loved it, got to see both parents every day, spend lots of time together. It was good. And I got to watch Garth become the father he wanted to be.

G: In our region, in Oklahoma, life was what people may call "traditional," where the female runs the house, raises the kids, and the guy goes off to work. That's how it was with my grandparents, and that's how it was with my parents. But being the father of three daughters, I couldn't understand that. I always told my girls, "If you get the job, and you guys have kids, he can stay home. Let's make sure that you're also getting the most out of your time down here on this planet." So, really quickly there were a lot of ideas that were starting to contradict each other.

TRISHA YEARWOOD: Garth wanted to be there for his girls like his parents had been there for him, but at the same time, he wasn't a typical kind of parent. It's the way he approaches a lot of things, from business to raising kids. He asks the same question: *Why does it have to be done that way, just because that's how it was always done in the past?*

G: My girls were living in a very traditional environment, but with a dad that was encouraging them to question things. Pull back, ask questions, don't accept things just because they're easy. If it's something you love, explore it. If there's something inside of you that's screaming to get out, let it out. We're on a farm; we're here. "You want to play football? Okay." We get the pads, helmets. And,

man, you talk about crying, tears, laughing. "You want to drive a bulldozer? I know you're only twelve, but jump up here. Let's go over what we're doing." They were driving tractors. They were working on the farm.

TED LARKIN: I was kind of couch surfing, and the kids were around a lot. I think I got there right before Christmas 2000, which was Garth's first Christmas alone. We did the midnight run to Walmart and bought a fake Christmas tree and all kinds of stuff, and we decorated.

G: Sandy and I alternated holidays. So, if you had the kids last Christmas, you weren't going to have them this Christmas. If you had them last Thanksgiving, you weren't going to have them this Thanksgiving, that kind of thing. Not easy to get used to. But what you come to find out is that birthdays, holidays, well, they're just dates in a calendar. You can celebrate them the next day or the day before. Or you can do what we did: If you didn't have them on Christmas Day, then your Christmas was five days long, starting on the 26th. It's Christmas week, where every day it's Christmas. It was great. But it was for me as much as them, for my own heart, because I'd never spent Christmas by myself, ever, and that's what

you have to be ready for as a divorced parent. That's one of the hard things you look at. And I looked at it that first year in Oklahoma.

TED LARKIN: I can't imagine going through the things that he did right then. He's learning to be a single dad, he's learning to be without his mom, he's learning to live without touring. Man, that would be too much for most people.

G: Raising those girls was going to be the greatest joy and the greatest heartache. It's just the nature of parenting. But those fourteen years of my life are the ones I'll always remember. It was life at its best. I learned to be a dad, my girls got to know me, and I'd never for one second regret walking away from a career in order to find all of that. But the first part of it was pretty hard.

BRYAN KENNEDY: A lot of people leaned on him up to that point. He's the star. He's the one everybody goes to. But when he has a problem? I bet he felt alone. He's the most genuine person I've met in the entertainment world, but he was in a new situation. Trisha Yearwood was the difference in his life. He can

TRISHA YEARWOOD WAS THE DIFFERENCE.

—Bryan Kennedy

always be himself around her. It would take them some years, but the greatest thing he ever did is marry Trisha.

G: There was no manual for what I was looking to build. The big thing for me, the savior that was on the horizon for me, would be Trisha, because she's going to come in, and these girls are going to not only have a companion that is not their mom or their dad, but they're going to have an example that lives with them. How to treat people, how to be yourself, how to be independent. That little yellow house was going to change when she walked into it. We were all going to change when she walked into that house.

MAKING A
FAMILY

CHAPTER TWO

SO, YOU FIND YOURSELF DIVORCED, a single man in Oklahoma. Now, your best friend is in Nashville, and you're talking on the phone. And you start to wonder, what would it be like to date your best friend? Well, that sounds pretty cool. But before you can do that, here come the talks with your kids and their mom. And what you do is that do-unto-others thing. You're hoping if Sandy's going to start bringing a man around the kids, she'll talk to you about who this guy is and what he stands for. The girls were familiar with Trisha, and she was very familiar with the girls because she and I were on tour together every time one of the girls was born. So, she was someone we all already knew. And although it was still a challenge, already knowing her was a huge head start.

By the time Trisha first came to visit, in 2001, I was at the
edge of a new life with the girls. I was starting to find my way. But
her arrival signaled the real beginning. She brought a lot of light.
When Trisha and I started talking about what might come next,
she went, "I don't know anything about kids. But I'll try. I love
you that much…let's just start dating and see what happens."
So, we had Miss Yearwood out to the house for the first time.
I said to the girls, "Hey, Trisha's coming out. We need to get
a meal. Let's do something cool." The girls looked at me and said,
"Eat Like Dog Night!" I said, "No, no, no." But I got outvoted
three to one.

Eat Like Dog Night was this: You got the mildest pasta sauce,
cooked up some spaghetti. Then, when everyone was served,
you counted one-two-three, and everyone threw their forks
over their shoulder and started eating face-first. We loved it.
But for Trisha's first night? I couldn't stop it. This was going to
happen. So, Trisha's sitting on the end. August is sitting beside her.
Everybody throws their silverware and drops their faces in the
bowl, except Trisha doesn't,
and neither does August. I look
up, and August is on her feet,
going over to Trisha, and she
just plants Trisha's face in that
spaghetti. I'm going, "Oh, shit!"
But Trisha never misses a beat,
just reaches up and pushes
August's head right into her
bowl. Trisha and August have
been peas and carrots ever
since that night.

✱ ✱ ✱

G: When I first told Sandy, "Hey, look, can you keep the girls two nights in a row? Because Trisha's coming in on Friday night." She goes, "Yeah, I can do that." And then I said, "Look, I'll make you a promise." I told Sandy that if Trisha was there on a night the girls were there, I'd sleep on the couch. Trisha would sleep in the bedroom. The girls would sleep in their room. Sometimes the girls would come in and lie with me on the couch. But it was important for everyone to see that when you established the rules, you stuck to them, for respect. So, unfortunately, I slept on that couch a lot. It was just about being very open and honest about what was going on.

TED LARKIN: When Trisha would visit, I got kicked out to the saddle room. (laughs)

TRISHA YEARWOOD: I just loved my visits. Pretty soon I cut my dates to like forty a year, from two hundred a year. I was still releasing music, though, so I was living and working here in Nashville and then going out there to see them. But at some point we decided, okay, if we're going to really make a go at this, I have to be there. And I have to be in these girls' lives too. I can't just float in and then leave. I've got to commit or not. And that's a whole different story, because that was a huge change for me.

IT'S ABOUT BEING THERE

TED LARKIN: I can't imagine how hard that was for her.

TRISHA YEARWOOD: Garth at least had a tie to Oklahoma. I had no ties, not just then. And I didn't know how to leave Nashville. I wasn't retiring. I didn't know how to do it. But I also knew that I was in love with him. I had to be where he was. It was not really a choice. But it was a change, a big one. I loaded up my dog and drove out there. And thank God I did it. It was the best change ever.

G: I couldn't have done it. If I were Trisha, I just couldn't have done it.

TRISHA YEARWOOD: I think my idea at first was, okay, I'm going to go try this. Not having kids of my own, I didn't know what was ahead. But I learned quickly that it was about being there for everything. People always say, "Well, we spend quality time together when we see each other." It's like, no. It's about quantity. It's about being there all the time. And that was the decision, even if I didn't know that right away. If you would've told me I was going to live there for fourteen years, I probably would've said, "No, that's not possible. I can't go. I can't do that. I can't just leave everything I've worked so hard for."

G: Man, when Trisha moved there, it was crazy, because here's a celebrity that's not from here and somebody you never thought you'd see living in Oklahoma. And she's got to figure out her career—because I announced

ALL THE TIME. —Trisha Yearwood

my retirement; Trisha didn't. Right away she cut all her dates down, way down, so she could be there as a partner to me and a parent to those kids.

TRISHA YEARWOOD: I had that conversation in my head about leaving Nashville. Believe me, leaving Nashville was never my plan. Not in the beginning. "I can't go live in Oklahoma. What is happening?" But I did. And I made the best friends of my life. And I learned that these girls were a gift in my life I didn't even know I needed. And I got to see a different side of Garth. I got to know him in a way that I'm so grateful that I know him. I got to see Garth being a dad. Did he tell you about Honesty Club? He says he didn't know how to be tender. But I saw a lot of tender.

G: The Honesty Club? Well, you'd put a candle in the middle of the floor, usually the girls' bedroom. We'd all lie on our stomachs. Everybody would touch the candle, and someone would say, "What's said in the club…" And then all of us would say together, "Stays in the club." Now that you know that, I can't say anymore. [Smiles]

TRISHA YEARWOOD: It was so good. Sometimes it would start where there'd just be quiet. Nobody would be saying anything. It'd be everybody just laughing. And you'd think, "Well, not a lot's going to happen here." Then somebody would start crying, and something would come out. I loved it, because I was raised in a house with a dad I loved, who was my hero, but my dad was never, "Let's talk about your

THEY WERE PARENTS...
NO INSTRUCTION MANUALS.
—Chris Geissler

feelings." That was not my dad. To watch a man do that with his daughters was like… I just…It was unreal. I'm not the crier, either. Garth is. But thinking about it is going to make me cry.

G: There's a few things that are happening around this time, internet-based developments, MySpace, all this stuff is starting to happen. You're just watching it build. We knew they needed a place to talk about it—the drama, the pressure, the unfortunate truths, like teen suicide, addiction, etc. Here's the Honesty Club at work. Here's what we need to talk about. And they have a place to bring it to. You could talk about fears. You could talk about goals. A faith in a higher power. All right here at this candle.

TRISHA YEARWOOD: I don't know where he came up with Honesty Club, but I think it should be in parenting books. It was really good.

G: My favorite thing about it—me and Trisha will agree on this—is that never once, never once did any of the girls ever come home from school and say, "Hey, Dad, you remember we said what's said in the club stays in the club? Well, my sister said this at school." Never once. Everything that was said at that candle stayed right there. It was just a chance to get it out, whatever they wanted to talk about, because when you talk about getting down on the floor with them, that's getting down on the floor with them. You give them that chance to say, "Hey, Dad, this happened." Okay, now let's address it.

TRISHA YEARWOOD: Garth had the girls question themselves. He challenged them. We didn't let them get away with anything. Our house was probably a stricter house in that regard, but now those girls, when the shit hits the fan, this is the guy they call. He went through it and earned something with those girls. It was an adventure at our house. It was fun. But there was also discipline. There were rules, because we *all* need boundaries.

TED LARKIN: Those girls are tough. They're not afraid of anything. (laughs)

TRISHA YEARWOOD: If Garth had them on the night before Crazy Hair Day at school, he would be sitting on the floor with a can of Dippity-Do, doing their hair, so in the morning when they got up, they'd have crazy hair. Every single night when they went to bed, they got a story, and it was not a story in a book. It was a story that Dad made up on the spot. Like when him and his brother Kelly invented the wide-mouth bass!

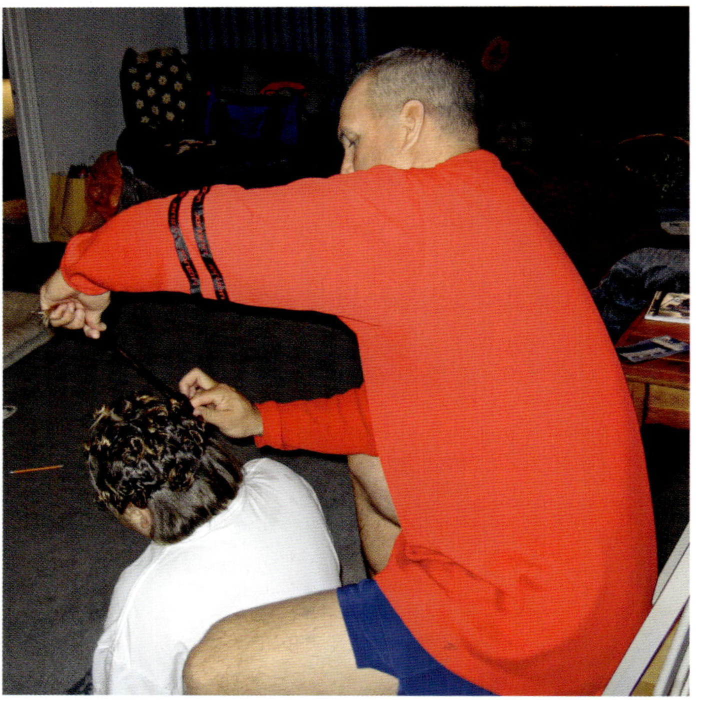

G: Every one of those stories was true. (laughs)

TRISHA YEARWOOD: You didn't want to miss those stories. *Every* story started with, "Me and your uncle Kelly…" They were amazing. There was a lot of tender. They knew whenever they needed him, he was there. And they still know that. That confidence in knowing he's there was forged during that time.

TED LARKIN: I watched Garth and Sandy try to be in the girls' lives together, as much as two divorced people could. Then Trisha came in, and I saw the demand on Sandy and Garth actually ease up when it came to those kids. Trisha really jumped in.

G: A lot of things got easier when Miss Yearwood arrived. She became family. I mean, the food alone! The girls will still talk about how much better it got when she showed up. They'll say, "When Trisha got there, the food changed, and we were so happy about that." For our fifteenth anniversary, we all got together and had Tyson Chicken Strips and boxed mac and cheese, because that was one of "Dad's meals."

TRISHA YEARWOOD: By the time I got there, Garth had his three or four things he'd make. He didn't have anybody helping. Nobody cooked for Garth and his girls. He had his standard things that they ate. His burritos were really good. [pause] But, yeah, the food did change when I showed up.

G: So much changed. So much. When Trisha got there, the adventure had really begun.

TRISHA YEARWOOD: At first it was, "What am I going to do with these girls?" As time went on, it was, "What am I going to do without them?"

TED LARKIN: Trisha showed up in the nick of time. That whole family became a part of the community. They would meet Chris and Lisa Geissler, along with Joe and Kim LeFlore. Garth and Trisha would be able to say, for the first time, that they had friends who weren't in the entertainment industry. They would parent together, learn together…no rules…just following their gut. The Geisslers and LeFlores had a front-row seat to watch Trisha and Garth find their life together. I would even go so far as to say this: The Geisslers and the LeFlores helped Garth and Trisha find that life.

WHEN TRISHA GOT THERE,
THE FOOD CHANGED. -g

FINDING A
COMMUNITY

CHAPTER THREE

BY THE TIME TRISHA WAS THERE, WE BOTH knew that our life as a family was going to be shaped by our community, by being a part of that community. We couldn't let our lives be defined by what we'd done in the past—it had to be about who we were right then, right there. All of the girls, Taylor, August, and Allie, played soccer. They went from being homeschooled into Rejoice Elementary into, eventually, public schools, but soccer was the constant. And on the sidelines some friendships were born that would matter more to us than I can tell you. The LeFlores and the Geisslers, these two families in particular, they raised the girls with us. They had kids the same ages, and we all just kind of lived those fourteen years together.

What is it about those kinds of friendships? Maybe it's some confirmation that, no matter what, you're taken care of. I couldn't have scripted this myself and come up with such a great story of a group of people finding one another. The love that flowed between those three families that met on the soccer sidelines was, and is, as deep as anything I've known. It felt like it was our fate to end up in each other's lives. We did everything together: birthdays, Halloween, Christmas. We played cards into the morning hours, worked on the farm, tried to get the kids into bed, let them stay up, played basketball, took walks, built things and broke things, laughed and cried. We did it all together.

✳ ✳ ✳

LISA GEISSLER: The soccer coach had said, "I just need to let you know we have someone you might recognize among our parents, and we ask that you be discreet." But people were like that anyway. Everyone was sweet. Yes, there were people who would hang out at Reasor's, the grocery store, hoping to meet Garth, but everyone was respectful. Later on, when we went out of town to games, that was sometimes different. Eventually, after knowing them a while, people would go, "You know him?" I'm like, "Yeah. I know him." "Wow. What's that like?" "Just like you and me sitting right here right now having a conversation." And that's exactly what it was like, from the beginning.

L to R: Kim and Joe LeFlore, Lisa and Chris Geissler, Trisha, and Garth

G: The parents are bringing their own chairs, watching the practices, talking. And there was a woman there at one of those early practices who had a football. But she's just sitting in her chair. I said, "Hey, a football, cool." And I started playing catch with another dad. I could kind of tell this pissed her off but wasn't sure why. I saw her the next night at soccer, though, so I said, "Can

NO, IT CAN'T BE THE SAME GUY.

—Joe LeFlore

I guess something?" She says, "Yeah." I said, "You were mad at me yesterday, weren't you?" She goes, "Yeah, I was." I said, "Was it because I took the ball and started playing catch with another dad and not you?" She goes, "You're damn right it was." So, me and her started playing catch. I came home, and on the phone that night told Miss Yearwood, "You're going to love this woman." That was Lisa Geissler.

CHRIS GEISSLER: My wife came home from soccer practice and goes, "You'll never guess who I met tonight." And I'm like, "Yeah? Who?" And she says, "Garth Brooks." I said, "Really?" And she's like, "Yeah, he's a really nice guy. I threw a football around with him." What?! Well, that's kind of cool, right? Then, sure enough, I took our Taylor to that next practice, and there's this guy kind of just standing off by himself. He's in a ball cap, Carhartts, and work boots.

JOE LEFLORE: Once your kids are selected for a soccer team, you get a list of the parent contacts. We saw it, and one name was Troyal Garth Brooks. We're like, "No, it can't be the same guy."

KIM LEFLORE: And then Joe went to the first day of practice, and he called me and goes, "That's who it is. It is Garth Brooks." I went to practice the next day and, yeah, he just came walking out on the field with Taylor, like every other dad. From then on, he was always there. Practices and games.

JOE LEFLORE: I tried to give him space. I didn't want to be the person that was just all in his face. But then he introduced himself. The coach was talking to everybody, collectively, explaining how everything was going to run, and I remember him shaking everyone's hand and introducing himself.

G: Taylor, our oldest, was on the Goal Girls, and that team had a kid named Shelby. Shelby's dad, Joe, was a fireman, and his wife, Kim, was a dental hygienist. And I'm sitting there talking to him like I'm his brother. We were pretty much raised the same way. I came home, called Trisha, and said, "There's this couple called the LeFlores. I don't know what it is about them, but we're going to have to get to know them."

JOE LEFLORE: It was still kind of a gradual thing. We just kind of gravitated toward each other over the course of practices. Garth was always inquisitive, like, "What do you do?" In a good way, you know? It made you feel comfortable. He would initiate conversations. I'm a firefighter, so we talked about that. But I'll tell you, I didn't say, "So, Garth, what do you do?" You know? As if I wasn't listening to his music in my truck? (laughs)

TRISHA YEARWOOD: One of the first times that I came to Oklahoma—I don't remember if it was when I moved there; I think it was just a visit—Ted [Larkin] picked me up and dropped me off at a soccer practice. That's when I met Lisa Geissler. And I'm like, okay, this is baptism by fire. You're not just going to come into town and hide out. You're actually going to somebody's side yard where there was a soccer field, and you're going to jump right in it. Lisa Geissler and Kim LeFlore were soccer moms, and they just embraced me.

JOE LEFLORE: I was either picking up or dropping off my son at school. I must have been picking up, because they were walking into the building. But I saw Garth walking toward me, and there was a woman with him. I'd never

met her. She had her glasses on and a ball cap, so you wouldn't have picked her out of a crowd. He walked up to the truck, and I rolled my window down. He said, "Joe, this is Miss Trisha. Trisha, this is Joe." Shook hands, and that's how I met Trisha Yearwood.

BLESSINGS COME IN THE THINGS YOU DON'T PLAN. —g

KIM LEFLORE: The first time we went out to dinner with Garth and Trisha, it was at Mary's Italian, and that was just a thank you because Garth had been watching the kids after my father died. It was a tough time, and this really helped us. But the first time the six of us went out, I think, was P.F. Chang's. We decided we were going to start going out to eat as three couples every so often, without kids. But we're still getting to know each other, that kind of deal. We ordered, and everybody was very polite. We leave P.F. Chang's, and one of the guys, I don't know if it was Joe or Garth or who, but someone said, "Those were great lettuce wraps, but I'm starving." So, we ended up at a place called the Pie Hole and ate pizza.

JOE LEFLORE: We're in the parking lot *after* our first dinner out as three couples, and someone finally had to say it, you know? "I'm starving! Let's go eat." Our friendships might have really kicked in right about then.

KIM LEFLORE: We hit it off. It was just easy. I remember we were at the yellow house one night after that, and we were having a bonfire with the kids. We were roasting marshmallows and stuff. I couldn't believe the amount of marshmallow bags…everywhere. Why so many? We were never gonna be able to eat that many marshmallows. Just then, Garth hit our son, Wes, in the chest with a marshmallow. Wes didn't know what to do, and then, "thunk," Garth hits Wes with another marshmallow. This time, Wes picked it up and chunked it right back at Garth. Everyone grabbed a bag, and it was game on! I remember I beaned Trisha with a marshmallow…

TRISHA YEARWOOD: Right in the face! (laughs)

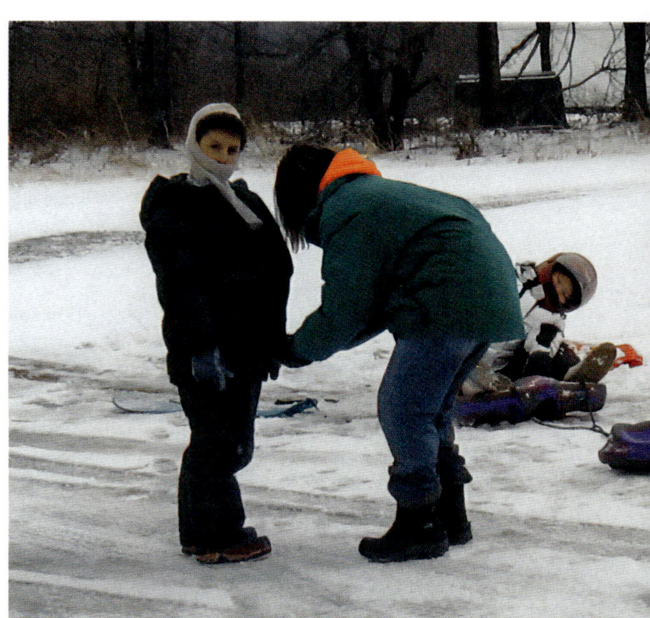

50

KIM LEFLORE: …and she was like, "Okay, we're going to be friends."

LISA GEISSLER: I feel like we all just clicked. It's like you go, "Yep, I would love to throw the football with him again and just sit and talk and chit chat," and then it turns into, well, you're really in one another's lives. The kids brought us all together. It goes from, "Oh, man, Auggie loves Taylor, and Taylor loves Shelby," into, all of a sudden, "Okay, we get to have this extended family." We didn't miss birthdays. We celebrated Christmas together.

G: Sometimes the blessings come in the things you don't plan. I was so focused on raising my girls, on Trisha's arrival, this new situation. But then I started to see a life take shape, the arrival of these friends who would, in the end, be friends for life.

LISA GEISSLER: We didn't just drop our kids off and go—we were there and watching it all happen and being present. How long did it take for us to watch anything with sound on the television when we were all together? There'd be baseball games on, and there'd be no sound. Garth and Trisha were so present for the kids, and for us. I always wondered, "When he's onstage, can he see everybody from up there?" Because sometimes people go, "Oh yeah, he's pointing out here, but he can't really see us." Well, I got invited later, years later, to take pictures from the stage during the concert.

THEY SAW US.
EVERY ONE OF US.

—Lisa Geissler

And I'm like, "Wow, he can see every face and every sign." He and Trisha were like that for us, for the kids, for the people in our community. They saw us. Every one of us.

TRISHA YEARWOOD: These four people were the people that we kind of like let into the inner circle, and in a way that we hadn't before. These friends weren't in the music industry. Being in the music industry, being an artist, is often all about you. So, it was cool for us to have friends that weren't from that background.

BRYAN KENNEDY: I think Garth and Trisha both enjoyed these new friends because they're great people. But they were also great people who had no idea about the music business. They didn't know one producer, didn't know one Nashville guitar player, they didn't have a cousin who sings or a brother who tap dances. These were good people with normal lives. I think Garth and Trisha really needed that. It was a beautiful thing, and still is.

TRISHA YEARWOOD: What we shared was the place, the soccer fields, the schools, kids. Lisa and Kim were my two girlfriends that were there for it all. We would walk on the farm, on that four-mile hike. I would listen to them talk about their lives and their kids. I learned about having kids that age from them, and I could ask them questions because I was still learning my way. And it was wonderful. Whatever they thought we gave to them, they gave back to us tenfold.

CHRIS GEISSLER: For years we had conversations around the table, these three families. We found out very quickly that Garth and Trisha are very much in touch with their upbringings and what shaped who they are. And they stay very true to that.

TRISHA YEARWOOD: In that time, I was going to lose both my parents. But because I wasn't on the road, I got to spend a lot of time

THEY DIDN'T KNOW
ONE PRODUCER.

—**Bryan Kennedy**

with my family that I probably wouldn't have otherwise. I would've just been gone all the time. So, I don't have any regrets. When I moved to Oklahoma, Garth said, "I'm going to make sure that you see your folks as much as you would see them if you lived in Nashville." He flew them out all the time. We went to see them a lot. It was like he made it work for me as best he could. So, I had my family, and I got to see them a lot in an important time. But then I got another family, and that included people I never would have known if I hadn't moved out

Garth and Jack Yearwood

Trisha with her father Jack Yearwood

THE PEOPLE IN OKLAHOMA WILL
CHANGE YOUR LIFE. –g

there to Oklahoma. I went to every soccer game and every soccer practice, where some friendships started that would matter more to me than I ever could have imagined.

G: So, now the new girlfriend started to come to the soccer games. "Holy shit. That's Trisha Yearwood at our kid's soccer game! I'm going to go up and talk to her." But at the same time, the girls' mom was there. And damn it, the thing I'm most proud of, I think, is how that little tri-community of Collinsville, Owasso, and Claremore took such great care of Trisha and the girls' mom, in this wonderful balance of *no one gets paid more attention to than the other.* Everyone was made to feel welcome.

TRISHA YEARWOOD: Sandy set that example, too. She took good care to make it all about the kids. There was no drama on the sidelines, ever.

G: Maybe the biggest cheerleader that just made my heart swell was Sandy's dad. He treated Trisha like she was his own daughter and really showed everyone how it could be. He kind of led everything.

TRISHA YEARWOOD: Sandy's dad was so kind to me. He'd come up at a soccer game, put his arm around me, like he was saying, "This family is moving forward through divorce and will come out the other side a family." I mean, I know it sounds like it couldn't even be true. It sounds like if you wrote this in a script, people would go, "That would never happen."

G: That's Oklahoma. When people go, "What do you love about Oklahoma?" I say, "You know what? I'm not sure there's a lot of things to see. But the people there will change your life."

53

I'LL ALWAYS REMEMBER WALKING DOWN THE STREET, THE SMELL IN THE AIR, AND SHEETS OF PAPER FLOATING IN THE SKY.
—Warren Zanes

WARREN ZANES: I was in Brooklyn on September 11, 2001. Long before the sun set that day, the people of New York City were telling their stories of what they experienced, the details, what ended for them, what began. The power of story, as both an effort to understand the inexplicable and an instrument of healing, was evident. You told your story to your neighbor, listened to theirs. People did it by instinct.

As so many people have recalled over the years, that September 11 was a beautiful day. A clear, blue sky signaled so much that was good, and then, not even mid-morning, everything was thrown off-balance. My then-wife and I were celebrating our second anniversary. Though most businesses closed, the restaurant where we had reservations early that evening remained open. I'll always remember walking down the street, not saying much, a smell in the air that would linger for a month, at least, and the sheets of paper floating in the sky. They weren't torn pieces, but full sheets, from desks, printers, shelves, spread across that beautiful blue.

It was an experience that made a lot of people think about what mattered to them, where they wanted to be, who they wanted to be with. Community mattered. Seeing friends mattered. Having your kids close mattered. I remember talking with Garth one day, and 9/11 came up. I told him about my experience of the day. What I didn't know was that he, too, had a story, that he, too, was in New York City that day.

G: It was me, Bob Doyle, Karen Byrd, and Judy Cummings, a schoolteacher from the Nashville area. I knew Judy because I'd gone to her classroom to read to the kids.

KAREN BYRD: Judy Cummings taught at an elementary school in Lebanon, Tennessee, but Garth asked her to come with us to New York. I think it was her first time visiting the city.

BOB DOYLE: We were up there for Read Across America. Garth had been involved in that for years, going into schools to read to students, promoting literacy. He always liked doing it. That year, they asked him to be the national spokesperson.

KAREN BYRD: We were in Manhattan to do promotional photos for Read Across America. It was a beautiful morning, gorgeous.

G: I loved going to Judy Cummings's classes. We did it for so many years, they contacted Bob Doyle and said, "We'd like to talk to him about being a national spokesperson," which was a joy and an honor. So Read Across America needed a picture to put on posters, a photograph of the artist with a truly diverse group of children. New York City's going to be the place. The photograph's going to be taken on September 11, 2001. We come in September 10. I'd been living in Oklahoma for, what, a year and a half?

BOB DOYLE: We were just getting ready to release "Beer Run" as a single, I remember that. A George Jones duet was a really big deal for Garth. We're talking about one of his heroes.

KAREN BYRD: I'd been working for Bob Doyle and for Garth throughout the '90s, then moved over to Capitol.

G: When I retired, I asked Karen if she'd consider leaving Capitol and setting up her own PR company, working from home so she could be with her daughter. I was happy when she agreed to do that. So, when Read Across America asked me to be a spokesperson, we called Karen.

BOB DOYLE: I'll never forget when things changed that morning.

WE HEARD THE SECOND PLANE HIT. –g

G: We were driving downtown and noticed between the buildings—it looked like it was about thirty stories up—that smoke was just bellowing out across the opening where you look down the avenue. Somebody said, "What is that?" Eric was our driver. And Eric was a sweetheart, great sense of humor, and he goes, "Well, I don't know, but I'm going to guess that's New York City smog." We all laughed. Then we made a left, went about a block, stopped, and saw all the people on all four corners looking up, pointing, and then we heard the second plane hit. But we still didn't know what was going on, didn't know about any planes.

KAREN BYRD: It was a full day that was planned, and another to follow. Garth was scheduled to do the promotional things, photo and video, then a luncheon that the NEA had arranged with editors of some family, parenting, and education magazines. In the evening we were supposed to take the chartered plane to Washington, D.C., where he was going to receive an award from ASCAP.

BOB DOYLE: We were pulling into the photo shoot when we heard on the radio that a plane had hit one of the Twin Towers. At first, they said it was a small, single-engine plane. Then they corrected themselves, saying, no, it was a commercial jet.

G: We pulled into the photo shoot, heard that on the radio, and Bob Doyle, sitting right next to me, retired Air Force pilot, he just said, "Terrorists." And I'm like, "Not here, not in the States."

KAREN BYRD: I grew up outside of Philadelphia. My parents still live in the house I grew up in. So, I'd gone up for the weekend, left my daughter with my parents, and met the others on the 10th. We stayed at the Essex House, right off Central Park. The next morning, we were in the car, heading to the studio, listening to the radio, 1010 WINS, when we heard the report about a plane flying into the World Trade Center.

BOB DOYLE: It was a matter of taking very little information and putting it all together, and still being unsure of exactly what was going on.

KAREN BYRD: By the time we arrived at the studio, we learned about the second plane. At that point, we knew something was terribly wrong. But no one knew exactly what to do. I remember ironing Garth's shirt, like somehow he's going to still do these promos. I don't know what we were thinking or what I was thinking. I called my husband. At least I was able to use my cell phone. I was able to connect. A lot of people couldn't. I called my parents. They were just trying to figure out ways to get us home. Garth, Bob, and Judy had flown in on a charter, which was at Teterboro Airport. Then, at some point, we heard about the plane hitting the Pentagon. So, it's just gone from worse, to worse, to just surreal. So we thought, okay, what do we do?

G: They're getting the kids in line and everything, preparing for this photo shoot. Me and Bob walk outside. I'm looking at him, saying, "Bob, we need to get down to

IT JUST WENT FROM WORSE, TO WORSE, TO JUST SURREAL.

—**Karen Byrd**

wherever this is happening." Karen's inside talking to them, and she ends up being the one that has to deliver the message: "Look, maybe we don't do this photo today. We'll come back." They weren't happy with it; they wanted to get the photo done. But something was going on, and we couldn't figure out what it was. Then Eric, who was driving us, said, "Hey, they're telling everybody to get out of the city."

BOB DOYLE: They were closing bridges and tunnels.

KAREN BYRD: My brother was working for the Pennsylvania state police at that time. He was called immediately, stationed at a tunnel on the turnpike, just sort of watching for…who knows what we were watching for, right? But any sort of attempt at attacking the infrastructure. So, we were trying to leave but couldn't get out. Eventually we got on the New York Thruway, going north. It was really, really strange seeing police cars and state trooper cars at the exits.

G: Every bridge we passed either had a police or military presence. We ended up driving an hour and a half, two hours north of New York, crossing the river there, and then coming back down. We stopped at a McDonald's before we crossed the bridge, and we're standing in line and everybody's talking about it. This is where we're finally getting the information. There are people in line that have the dust on their shoulders, who were somewhere in the blocks around the buildings when one went down. That's how we kind of learned. When we got back to Teterboro, of course all the flights were grounded, but it was the first time you could look across the water and see where the two towers had been. Now it was just smoke billowing out.

KAREN BYRD: My parents were like, "Can you get here?" My dad's going, "I'll drive Garth back to Oklahoma." So, we're just trying to figure out what to do.

YOU COULD ONLY SEE WHERE THE TWO TOWERS HAD BEEN. —g

G: Karen's family is from Philadelphia, so Eric was sweet enough to say, "I'll drive you to Philadelphia. That way, at least you'll have a place to stay, a place to sleep." Karen's parents were fantastic.

KAREN BYRD: Once we were able to get to Philadelphia, we checked the others into a hotel, a Hampton Inn, I think. I stayed at my parents' house and, thankfully, got to see my daughter, Olivia. The next morning, the 12th, Bob Doyle called me, and he's like, "Listen, Judy's in tears here at the hotel. Maybe we could come over and see you." So, I went to pick up Judy and Bob, but Garth was coming out of the hotel too. So, we all went back to my parents' place, just to be together. Bob needed a battery for his watch. I drove Judy and him over to the mall. Garth stayed back. I remember one of my mom's neighbors called, and she was like, "Do you want to take a walk?" Mom said, okay, and evidently my mom, her friend, and Garth went for a walk around the neighborhood, with Garth pushing Olivia around in her stroller.

G: They let us camp out. Karen's parents really opened their home to us. We needed it just then, like people all across the country. Then Mike Green, who we leased the plane from, called and said, "Hey, man, I actually have a tour bus here. It's mine. I'll come up to Philadelphia and grab you." So, he drove up, picked us up, and drove us back.

BOB DOYLE: I can still see all the details, every place we stopped on our way back home. It's a time you remember better than others, and it brought the group of us very close together.

KAREN BYRD: Garth and Bob insisted that I have the state room at the back of the bus, me and my daughter. When we eventually got back to Nashville—I'll always remember this—Garth walked off the plane with my daughter and handed her to my husband and said, "This little candle is the only thing that's been good about the last couple days." It was an experience that has bonded us all for some time, just as it's bonded Americans together. Fortunately, I got to be with my daughter and my parents, and then eventually got to get home to my husband.

But I had family in the middle of it all. The rest of them did not, right? Until they could get home. It affected us all differently.

G: I'm sure what 9/11 did to us it did to most everybody. All the sudden you're thinking, "Well, how do I want to spend the rest of my life?"

KAREN BYRD: In the months after we got back, Read Across America was back on, and Garth said, "Let's really do it; let's read across America." We started on *Good Morning America*, did Nashville, Los Angeles, Tucson, Oklahoma City, and, for our last stop, Clarksdale, Mississippi, which at the time had the highest illiteracy rate in the country. In Clarksdale, he read to a second-grade class. They were

THAT TIME PLANTED A SEED THAT MADE ME WANT TO **DO A CAREER SHIFT.**

—Karen Byrd

all decked out in white shirts and black cowboy hats with red bandanas, and they sang "We Shall Be Free" to him before he read. It was really very moving. Judy went with us on that whole trip. It was really special, all of us back together. But I'll tell you, that time planted a seed that made me want to do a career shift. It took several years to figure out how to do that, but that planted the seed. A few years ago, I started working part time at the school where I'm now, working as a reading interventionist. Just this year, during Read Across America Week, I asked Garth if he would come and read to our school. And he did. He came to the school. That's full circle, and that's how lives can change.

G: How do you want to spend the rest of your life, and *who* do you want to spend the rest of your life with? And maybe it's time to take a really strong step toward getting that done. What you think about when that kind of tragedy happens, after the families directly affected by loss and grief, is what matters to you. On 9/11, I checked on my children, and then I was just trying to find Trisha. She was on the West Coast, which I knew. But, if you remember, everybody thought Los Angeles was going to be next. And most people couldn't get through to anybody. The feeling? Life is unpredictable. Don't wait. I knew then that it was time. If she'd have me.

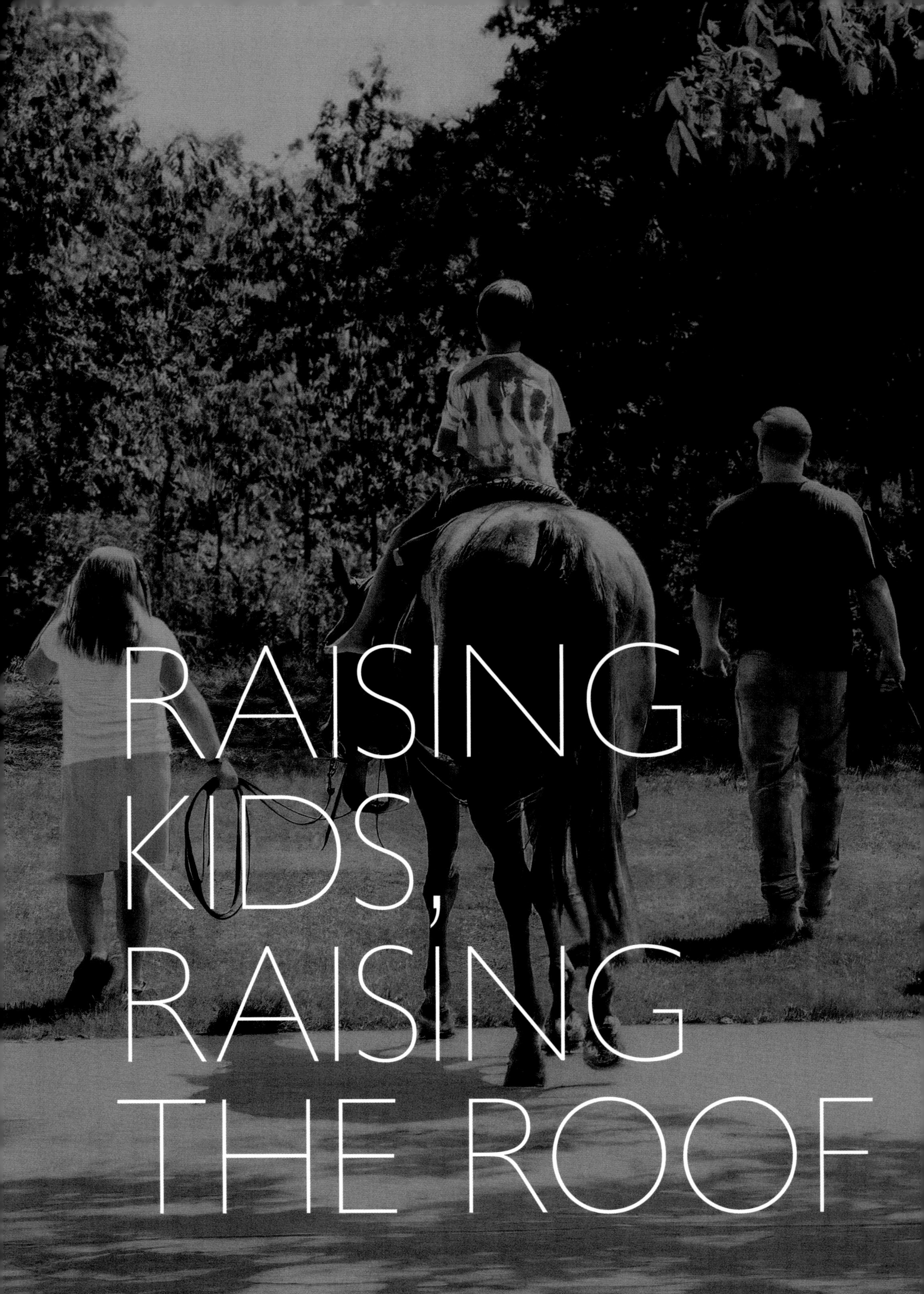
RAISING
KIDS,
RAISING
THE ROOF

CHAPTER FOUR

FOR A TIME THERE, IT GOT DARK, AND I got really lost. But now I was into the sunlight of it all. My life in Oklahoma had become the life I knew best, with a lot of help and a lot of love from the people around me. In many ways, I'd kind of stopped being Garth Brooks and became more "Taylor's dad," or "August's dad," or "Allie's dad." Garth and Trisha were just another couple of parents. We brought the halftime snacks, stayed up late doing homework, and carried soccer balls.

L to R: *Trisha, Lisa Geissler, and Kim LeFlore*

For Trisha's part, most of her friends up to that point worked for her, which was normal in our business. So, now, for her to have two girlfriends who were never in the Nashville loop, one of them a physical therapist from Wisconsin, the other a dental hygienist from Oklahoma? Those three became inseparable. The LeFlores have two children. Shelby played with Taylor, and Wes was their son. And then the Geisslers had two children. T-bone played with August. T-bone's name is Taylor, but since there were so many Taylors, you've got a T-bone. And then Haley was underneath, and she ended up playing with Allie, who was around the same age. These are the sweetest people. So, any Friday night or Saturday night we didn't have the kids, we would sit at the table, the three couples, and just play cards but never ever keep score. We'd just talk about parenting; we talked about marriage, we talked about life. When we goofed around, it was fun. When we worked…it was serious fun!

* * *

LISA GEISSLER: We're chopping down trees. We're blazing trails. I mean, Garth was probably the hardest-working retired person that you would ever meet! He got up, took kids to school, and then came home and put on the Carhartts. He'd be out there doing stuff like making trails for us to walk on out at the farm.

CHRIS GEISSLER: When it started out, the girls had a three-mile trail. And then Garth was like, "I think I can cut a five-mile trail that Trisha, Kim, and Lisa can walk." And then, all of a sudden, we had a seven-mile trail.

G: Trisha and her girlfriends did these three-day walks for Susan G. Komen and the Breast Cancer Foundation. Three days, sixty miles, raising money for cancer research. It's like doing a marathon—you have to train. So, we cut trails for them…roads, actually. [*Chuckles*]

KIM LEFLORE: If the kids weren't playing soccer, me, Lisa, and Trisha were walking. I remember we did our first three-day, and at the end of it we were like, "We'll never do this again." And next thing you know, we were signing up for another one, camping in a little tent and bathing in a little portable shower. Without a doubt we had so, so much fun. We made so many memories on those walks. Raised a lot of money for cancer research. But, yeah, we trained.

YOU DON'T JUST GET OUT OF BED ONE MORNING AND **WALK TWENTY MILES.**

—**Trisha Yearwood**

TRISHA YEARWOOD: We had to train—you don't just get out of bed one morning and walk twenty miles a day for three days back-to-back! When they're over, you swear you can't do another, but we will never forget those experiences… and we kept coming back for more.

KIM LEFLORE: Out here, walking the woods, there's critters. There are mountain lions, coyotes, rattlesnakes, different things. So, Trisha would always bring a little handgun just in case something attacked us. And we used to laugh, because Lisa was the only runner in our group. So, Trisha always joked, saying, "All we have to do is shoot Lisa in the foot and we'll be fine." We were out there all the time, after work and evenings.

CHRIS GEISSLER: Yeah, the trails got longer, and that meant there were streams to cross. So then bridges got built.

L to R: Mandy McCormack, Kim LeFlore, Lisa Geissler, and Trisha

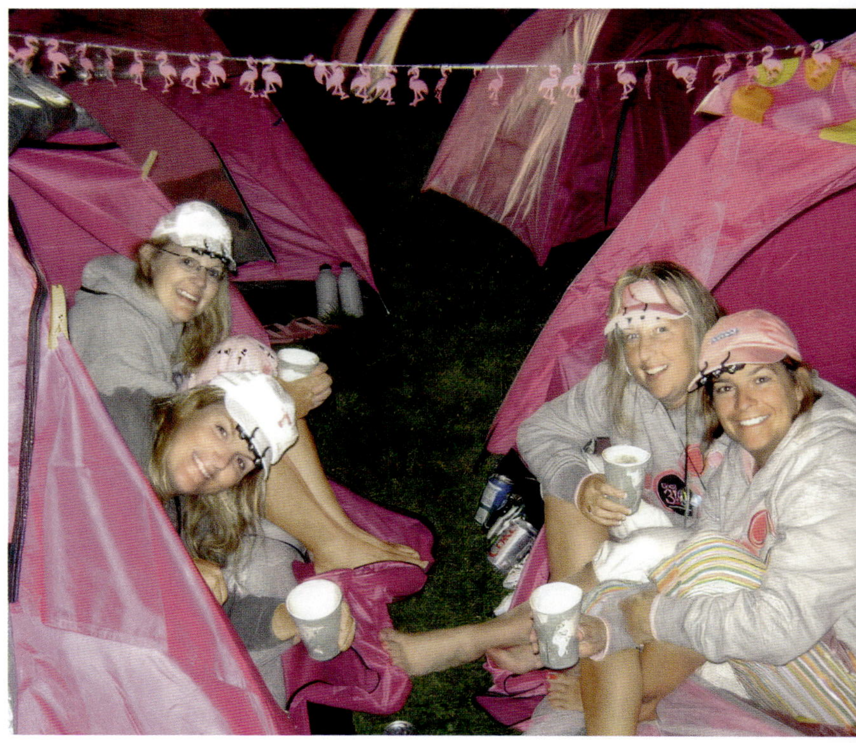

L to R: Beth Bernard, Trisha, Mandy McCormack, and Kim LeFlore

G: I love bridges. So, I build bridges, and I draw them all the time. I've been doing that for thirty years. Tension bridges, compression bridges, suspension bridges. What I like is they bring together two things that maybe aren't supposed to be coming together. So, I just love the whole symbolism of it. But we had a loop on the farm that was around four miles long, and Miss Yearwood and her girlfriends would always come home with muddy shoes because of this one place on the trail. I said, "You know what, we're going to build a bridge, because we need one for the tractors anyway *(wink)*."

JOE LEFLORE: If all I knew were the CDs in my truck, I wouldn't have expected Garth Brooks to be a bridge builder. But by the time he started that project, I had gotten to know him—and nothing would have surprised me.

G: I used it as an excuse to do some bonding with my girls, something that was more in my wheelhouse. I wanted to see how they'd do coming across to me, how they'd adapt to that. Because I was adapting to all this tender stuff, so I felt we should explore how they did on my side of things. In that way, it really was bridge building.

TRISHA YEARWOOD: I would say he was just being a father. Sometimes the father's tender, and sometimes the father is tough. It was all that at our house. It was fun, and there was discipline. Eat Like Dog Night, Honesty Club, bridge building, skateboards in the house. It was a balance.

G: So, we built that bridge as a father-daughter project. When I first told the girls we're going to do a project together, Miss Yearwood said, "Garth, I think they believe you're going shopping." But we ended up building a 56-foot compression bridge. The first thing we drive over it when it's done is a fully loaded dump truck. Me and the three girls. They'd shoot grade, pour concrete, torch cut metal, work with nail guns, and chop saws, everything.

NOTHING WOULD HAVE SURPRISED ME.

—Joe LeFlore

IF I'M PICKING A TEAM,
MY FIRST THREE PICKS
ARE GOING TO BE
THOSE GIRLS. —g

BRYAN KENNEDY: I liked that he went home and could see the sun set seven hundred miles away, the wind blowing, the trails they'd cut. You can't replace that stuff. That guy, you give him some Carhartts and Timberlands, and he's right at home.

G: All of them have a scar somewhere on their body from that four months of building. And they would have boys come visit. "Hey, Dad, can somebody come over?" I'd say, "Okay. Here's how it is. If he comes over, we're working two hours on the bridge, and then rest of the day you guys can do your thing." And Miss Yearwood can vouch for this: There wasn't a day that a boy came over when that boy didn't end up sitting under the shade, a bleeding nose or something while the girls worked. So maybe I didn't know a lot about being tender, but I do know that if I'm picking a team right now to get a job done, my first three picks are going to be those three girls, because they know work.

TRISHA YEARWOOD: It gave them confidence too, confidence to do almost anything. If you ask them today about something, they'll be like, "Yeah, we can do that. We built a bridge." Like, really, they say that now. It gave them a boost. It gave me that, too. I helped with that bridge. I learned to pour concrete and use a nail gun and all that stuff. It was a great. To me, this speaks to the hard part of being a parent. You push them, and none of us like to be pushed past our comfort zone, but that's usually where all those magic things happen in our lives.

LISA GEISSLER: But I guess the paradox was kind of like this: We did a lot of stuff together, but the beauty, for me, was that the relationship is not actually built around doing things. It's built around doing nothing.

OUR RELATIONSHIP WAS NOT BUILT AROUND DOING THINGS… IT WAS BUILT AROUND DOING NOTHING.

—Lisa Geissler

CHRIS GEISSLER: Just being together.

LISA GEISSLER: Because you've got these friends who are really in your lives, and it's like, okay, what are we going to do tonight? And sometimes it's plugging in a movie, watching it with a few of them while you're also listening to three other people in the room snore. It got comfortable.

JOE LEFLORE: Yes, there were rules. But it may have been hard to see the discipline from the outside, because Garth and Trisha also spoiled all of our kids. But by "spoiled" I mean that when they came out here, it was game on. Whatever the kids wanted to do, we did. Whether it was going to the lake and riding Jet Skis, tubing, fishing, jumping off the houseboat, or four-wheeling on the property.

KIM LEFLORE: Eat Like Dog Night. That alone was something my kids were never going to forget.

JOE LEFLORE: Eat Like Dog/Drown Like Cat Night—the "cat" part because they'd always run through the sprinkler or jump in the pool with spaghetti sauce all over their faces after eating like a dog. I wish I could put into words for you what it meant to them. Our kids had a wonderful, wonderful life being a part of Garth and Trisha's world. It's not the material things, but just to come out here and really be kids. When it'd snow, we'd hook the sleds up and drive them around the farm, pulling them behind the Jeeps. Just stuff that they wouldn't have had an opportunity to do otherwise—but it was all Norman Rockwell kind of childhood activities. Sweet, fun, healthy stuff, and lots of it.

KIM LEFLORE: I know our daughter has said many times that this is where her childhood was, out here at Garth and Trisha's house. This is where she grew up.

JOE LEFLORE: The kids were out here all the time. Even when we weren't here, the kids were out here. But again, you got to understand that for the first five years, they're living over there in the yellow house. And I don't think our kids really even understood who Garth was, who Trisha was. I can remember the first time Wesley saw Garth on television, I think it was one of those concerts on the aircraft carrier. Wes was little. He was watching it, and he turns around and goes, "That's Taylor's dad." Like he'd discovered something none of us were aware of. He was just in shock. I'm like, "Yeah, he's a singer. That's what he does."

G: I mean, I remember Joe LeFlore sitting there one time in the middle of a card game, and he goes, "Hey, Trisha, while you're up, would you grab me a beer?" She sets it down, and Joe starts laughing. "What is it?" He goes, "Fucking Trisha Yearwood brought me a beer!"

TRISHA YEARWOOD: I remember sitting there watching something with the sound down, and I'm like, "Joe, let's see your playlist." I look, and it's all Garth Brooks. I say, "Joe, come on." He's like, "But I love these songs." So, I think they allowed us to be regular people. The community saw us at the grocery store every week, saw us taking our kids to soccer or school, and saw us going to church on Sundays. So, I think at some point they just had to go, "Okay, this is who they are."

G: My favorite thing was when we'd get in a store and, because Trisha had her cookbooks,

FUCKING TRISHA YEARWOOD BROUGHT ME A BEER!

—Joe LeFlore

some lady would come up and go, "My husband loves your meatloaf but he's diabetic and he can't..." And Miss Yearwood would take her by the hand and say, "Substitute this, and then add this." I'd trail them with the cart and wait. It's the sweetest thing you can possibly do. Never once have I seen her slight somebody to save her own time. I just haven't seen it.

TRISHA YEARWOOD: Sometimes you'd go to the grocery store, go in and get your stuff, and leave. And then sometimes you'd go in the grocery store, and you would stay for hours. It'd be like a meet and greet. No rhyme or reason. It was like you just never knew what it was going to be. I've watched Garth talk for twenty minutes to somebody that just needed to talk to him. And yet, somehow, no matter our careers, we really became a part of that community.

G: They never once let you forget who you were, and they never once treated you like you weren't one of them. I don't know how they did that. But the impossible wasn't pulled off by us. The impossible was pulled off by them. And I'm talking about the people of Oklahoma, not just Joe and Kim and Chris and Lisa. Yeah, the impossible was pulled off by them.

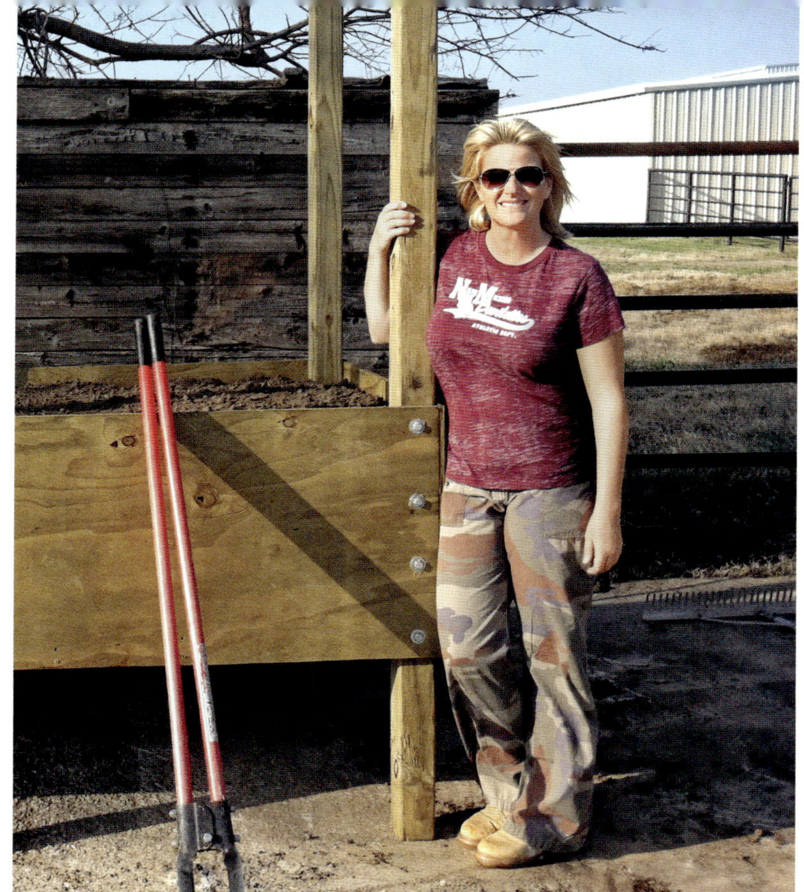

THEY ALLOWED US TO BE
REGULAR PEOPLE.

—Trisha Yearwood

MUSIC COMES CALLING

CHAPTER FIVE

I HAD FOUND THIS LIFE. THIS TIME IT WAS a life centered around my girls. And then Miss Yearwood came into it, bringing so much to us all. And then these new friends, the lifelong kind of friends, came into it. When I'd retired five years earlier, I didn't know what I would find. What I found was heaven…and then some, believe me. Things in that little yellow house were so damn good. Not always easy, but always good.

I also realized the music was going to carry on with or without me. Which is a good feeling, trust me. Just knowing the music was out there, still circulating, the songs still being passed from person to person. But I had no plans to dip my toe back in the music business. I wasn't going to tour, and I wasn't making new albums.

Miss Yearwood was just completing a show for CMT. I was with her. The producer of the show expressed that the network would like to do a show on my career in the '90s. I did the interview. And, honestly, it was fun to look back at the career. What was really fun, though, was looking back on the career from the outside. But what I didn't know was that a man named David Porter, who worked for the world's largest retailer at the time, saw the interview. It gave him an idea, and, though I had no way of knowing this, he was looking for me.

I HAD **NO PLANS** TO DIP MY TOE BACK IN **THE MUSIC BUSINESS.** —g

✳ ✳ ✳

G: One day in the yellow house, my phone rings…it's Pat Quigley. At this point, I haven't talked to Pat in four or five years. Phone rings, not a hello or anything. All I hear is, "Here's the deal…" I said, "Pat?" He goes, "The guys from Walmart are going to come out there to see you. I need you to take the meeting." I said, "Pat, I'm retired." "Would you just take the meeting?" I said, "Pat…" He goes, "Garth, I'm needing a yes here. Just take the meeting. What can it hurt?" So I said yes.

DAVID PORTER: I got to Garth through a man named Bill Lardie, a gentleman and a scholar. Bill knew Pat Quigley. But the first thing Bill Lardie told me was, "Well, Garth's retired." And I said, "Good, that means he's got time for lunch." I knew Garth was taking the kids to school and kind of hanging out on the sidelines during soccer and doing all the things that dads do. But Bill eventually got a hold of Garth, and we set a lunch. I drove over to Tulsa from Bentonville.

PAT QUIGLEY: Shortly after I called Garth, a few things started coming together: the idea of doing another *Limited Series* box set and the question of who to do it with. A man named Gary Severson was the Walmart executive who expressed interest in David Porter's vision of doing something special with Garth.

THEY HAD A
BIG IDEA
AND KNEW ONLY
GARTH
COULD PULL IT OFF.

—Pat Quigley

Bob Doyle and Garth

SOMETHING
TOLD ME THIS GUY
WASN'T DONE.
—David Porter

Walmart's music division was controlled by a company named Anderson Merchandisers, of which Bill Lardie was the president. So, Bill Lardie was very important in this, and he knew Garth was retired. They respected that, but they also had a big idea and knew only Garth could pull it off.

DAVID PORTER: We sit down to eat, and obviously the waitress and the servers and people that were there respected Garth's privacy. He said hi to everybody, so obviously they had seen him or he knew his way around there. I could tell it was just like he was almost another person in the community by that time. So, we had a little lunch. But I should say that growing up in Oklahoma myself, I was obviously a huge fan. Let's just start there. I believe the first time I ever saw Garth live would've been the Texas Stadium show. I went with a group of people, and it was just an amazing experience for all of us. But something in the CMT interview I saw told me this man wasn't done.

G: And so David Porter comes out and goes, "We want to do something that's totally exclusive with Walmart." I say, "David, I'm done." He says, "I understand you're done. We're not asking you to make any new music." I'm sure my face gave away my surprise. He waited a beat and then he said, "But do you have anything in the vault?"

DAVID PORTER: During that lunch, we just kind of got to know each other, with him emphasizing that he wasn't interested in doing anything while he was raising the kids, and me

letting him know that I thought that was what could make this opportunity unique. Because we really didn't need him to be on tour or create anything new. We just felt like, yeah, if he had some music in the vault, archived or something, that we could package, well…

L to R: Garth, David Porter, Kate Porter, and Trisha

G: I was thinking like, "There's generally a reason why this stuff's in the vault. It was either not good enough to make the record or it never got finished, right?" But then I remembered "The River" sat in the vault for three years. So, I told him we'd have a look.

DAVID PORTER: We felt like our fans and our shoppers and our customers were missing music from him.

G: So, we go in the vault and pick out about sixteen things. And I'll say this, vaults are funny. You listen back, and you can't remember why it got there in the first place. It's sounding pretty good to me! So, I got back to David and said, "Well, what are we talking here?

I still don't really know?" And that's where Pat Quigley comes in. Quigley thinks we should put a second box together, a second in *The Limited Series*.

JOE LEFLORE: I was seeing Garth all the time, doing family things, playing poker, working on the farm. As far as I could see, he was all the way out of music. You wouldn't have known he was talking about a new record of stuff that hadn't been released. I sure didn't, and he was standing right in front of me. I think once he made it about the kids, he didn't ever think to make it about himself in that way.

PAT QUIGLEY: When Garth retired, I pretty much retired too. But my phone still rang. And I got a call from the new chairman of EMI Capitol Worldwide in the London office. He said to me, "Would you go out and spend a day or two in L.A. with the new people at Capitol and explain what the Garth opportunities are going forward?" I'll do anything for Garth, so I said sure.

STORME WARREN: Pat Quigley was a guy that made pink ski boots fly off the shelf, plastic watches become a monster success. Everything Pat Quigley touched in business seemed to go very, very well.

PAT QUIGLEY: I wasn't there at Capitol for five minutes before we started talking about what business opportunities there were with Garth. And I said, "Well, the first thing I would work on is another box set. It's good for at least a million units." And the new guy at Capitol said to me, "That's the stupidest thing

IT'S HARD TO COMPETE
WITH FARM EQUIPMENT.

—Trisha Yearwood

I ever heard. No one's ever sold a million box sets." To which I said, "Are you actually the new president?" He goes, "Yeah." I said, "You're an idiot! Garth Brooks, your guy, sold 2 million box sets already."

BOB DOYLE: I think it happened pretty fast that Garth saw that the problems he had with his record label were, well, still problems.

G: After hearing about Quigley's conversation in L.A., I went to see Mike Dungan, head of Capitol Records in Nashville. I explain to Mike with this Walmart deal, you're going to move about 18 million units, over 2 million box sets. Dungan hesitated… then expressed his concern of pissing off the rest of retail. I explained this was found money, just stuff out of the vault. The conversation was short. It was just a stone wall. No.

STORME WARREN: It seemed like a win-win situation. But it wasn't, and I couldn't tell you why.

G: So, I go back to Walmart, and I tell David Porter, "Sorry, I can't do it." He goes, "What do you mean you can't do it? We've already got the ball rolling." I said, "I can't do it. I own my masters, but Capitol has the lease on them, and Capitol isn't interested. I have ten years left on my contract with them. You want to buy it out, you can. But I'm not paying for it. Which means

it's going to be money you're going to lose to make this deal happen." That's about when I got back on my tractor.

TRISHA YEARWOOD: Sometimes it's hard to compete with farm equipment. (laughs) Since Garth wasn't out there working in the music business every day, he didn't need to fight for this stuff. He had a life that was full, right there on a farm in Oklahoma. He could let the others figure out a few things for themselves.

PAT QUIGLEY: I think it becomes clear to Walmart and Anderson Merchandisers that, for a price, they could get rid of Capitol and release a box set exclusively with Walmart. The box set that the guy at Capitol thought couldn't sell a million, well, it sold 2.2 million in a very short time. I mean, Capitol really misunderstood what Garth meant. And the upshot of it all was that, very suddenly, Garth owned his masters ten years ahead of schedule.

G: I get a call from David Porter himself. And he says, "We're on." I said, "What?" Bob Doyle immediately calls me. He goes, "You kind of own your masters outright now." I said, "What do you mean kind of?" He goes, "Well, you're going to have to sign them over for Walmart's exclusive use for the period of the time we're working with Walmart." I said, "That's fine."

BOB DOYLE: It was an amazing moment.

> # ALL OF A SUDDEN, GARTH OWNED HIS MASTERS.
>
> **—Pat Quigley**

G: Wow. It's hard to convey the feeling of this, owning my own recordings outright. I was on the tractor when I heard the news. Now it was just a matter of getting recordings prepared for what would be called *The Lost Sessions*.

DAVID PORTER: Throughout all of this, I'd periodically drive over to see Garth. He was living in a really small place with his kids at that time. I think Sandy was on the other side of the property. I remember seeing him there and talking, kind of pinching myself because I'm like, "Here I am with Garth Brooks, someone that I really have a lot of respect for who is showing a lot of respect for me and my company." He's in this little house, and it was decorated with coloring book pictures everywhere, stuff the kids had done. I mean, the kitchen was wallpapered in coloring book pictures. Sometimes when I was there, the kids had some homework or something they needed help with, so it might take a minute. They came first. But I just remember one of those drives home after visiting him, thinking, "This is going to be an incredible experience if we're able to put it together."

GARTH WAS ALWAYS THERE
WHEN I LOOKED FOR HIM.

—Chris Geissler

G: *The Lost Sessions* meant going to Nashville, and Walmart knew I wasn't going to miss a soccer game. That's when they gave me use of the corporate jet.

CHRIS GEISSLER: You know, honestly, when Garth got to work on *The Lost Sessions*, I wouldn't say that I didn't notice it, but it wasn't a big deal, I guess. I didn't really feel like he was absent at any point during that time. He might feel differently. I don't know. Life carried on, and he was always there when I looked for him.

G: Get the girls up in the morning, make their lunches, take them to school, drive directly to the plane. An hour and forty-five minutes later, you are in the studio.

KIM LEFLORE: We didn't so much notice. You see, during *The Lost Sessions* he'd be back here for practice. And he didn't really talk about it. So even though he'd be gone during the day, we were all at work in those hours. So, he was at work during the day, but he's out there for soccer practice that evening.

G: Leave the studio in the afternoon, fly home, pick up the kids, homework, soccer, and put them to bed. Oh! Can't forget story time!

JOE LEFLORE: Maybe I should have been more inquisitive about that stuff. He's about as humble a person as you'll meet when it comes to his success. I guess I figured if he wants me to know, he'll tell me. We were focused on the kids, school, homework, practice. Life just carried on.

G: Next day, get up and do it again.

LOST
the sessions

THE LOST SESSIONS

CHAPTER SIX

SO WE WENT IN THE VAULT, AND THERE were these pieces, sometimes songs you'd totally forgotten about, that you could breathe life into. Some of these rough recordings weren't in a position to be released without some help. It was a mix of digging through the vaults, fixing some things, finishing some things. We got to take this walk through our history in the studio. But it was impressive what we were finding. That's the good thing about Allen Reynolds: just because a recording hadn't appeared on a record yet didn't mean it wasn't worthy. Sometimes it meant the song's time was still yet to come.

SOMETIMES, IT MEANT THE SONG'S TIME
WAS STILL YET TO COME. —g

GOOD RIDE COWBOY

By BRYAN KENNEDY, JERROD LEE NIEMANN, RICHIE BROWN & BOB DOYLE

G: Here's one with Richie Brown and Jerrod Niemann. Then you've got big Chuck, Bryan Kennedy, who's always great, and Bob Doyle. When Chris LeDoux passed, it was Bob who said, "Good ride, cowboy." And when I heard Bob say that, I was like, "Well, there it is. There's the title."

BOB DOYLE: I said to Garth, "Wouldn't that be a great metaphor for life? In the beginning, it's a literal thing where you say, 'Good ride, cowboy,' because they got bucked off or rode for eight seconds. But at the end of life, it means, 'Good ride, cowboy. You had a good life.'" Garth kind of went, "Yeah, I see that."

BRYAN KENNEDY: I was on the phone with Garth, who was out there in Oklahoma. That's how we wrote it. Bob had given him that line. I remember my phone beeping, because the battery was running out, and I'm think-ing, "Please, God, don't let this phone go dead!" I could hear Mandy McCormack in the background, throwing out lines from Chris's stuff.

G: Mandy threw a lot of ideas out for this one. She knows all the LeDoux songs inside and out. She was the one who loved that line from "Homecoming": "My, how the flowers grow." She grabbed stuff like "Running Through the Rain." We just started pulling lines from our favorite Chris LeDoux songs. And here it came: "Life is a highway."

BRYAN KENNEDY: Freaking Chris LeDoux. If I had a natural-born son, or nephews,

I would want them to be Chris LeDoux. He was just the nicest guy, a tough guy, talented guy. Another guy that just didn't believe you *couldn't* do it. It's just like, "I'm going to do it. I'm going to be a country music singer and a rodeo cowboy. I'm going to be a national champion, a bareback rider. I'm going to have a family, and I'm going to have kids. I'm going to sing for a living, and I'm going to travel the world. I'm going to jump over the drum kit and light off fireworks. And I'm going to be a gentleman." He went after it all and got it. I just loved being around him.

G: Jerrod and Richie came out to Oklahoma to write. So, we worked on that thing I had going with Bryan Kennedy. I had kind of a melody, but I thought it just didn't do anything. And Jerrod's looking at me going, "Are you just making this melody up right here? Or is this something else?" I said, "It's just what the words are leading me to." He says, "Just keep singing it." So, I kept singing it. And then when Jerrod started singing it, I was like, "Holy shit! That sounds really good when *he* sings it!" It was Jerrod who said, "I bet he crossed that River Jordan, with St. Peter on the other side…" I'm telling you, Jerrod is a monster writer and singer. It was a fun trip. A good collaboration.

HOLY SHIT! THAT SOUNDS REALLY GOOD WHEN *HE* SINGS IT! –g

JERROD NIEMANN: He calls one day, says, "What are you doing tomorrow? Want to come to Oklahoma?" What?! He flew us first class, and that was cool. We show up, and he's in the cowboy house, with all three of his girls sleeping in one room. Again—what?! But this is Garth Brooks. I felt like I was in a dream.

RICHIE BROWN: That trip to Oklahoma, the first thing that he pulled out for us when we got there was "Good Ride Cowboy." Right when he started going over it, I was thinking, "Man, this is a tribute to LeDoux." I mean, I kind of got tears in my eyes because I was like, "I can't believe we're about to be involved in this."

JERROD NIEMANN: We got a guy from Oklahoma, a guy from Texas, and a guy from Kansas— if we can't write a song about Chris LeDoux, I just don't know what we can do. But I'll tell you, my biggest fear was letting Garth down.

RICHIE BROWN: It's hard to talk about "Good Ride Cowboy" because I never knew if I was really allowed to say much, because Garth took his name off the song. But I know firsthand that song wouldn't have happened without him. It had a good start by the time it came to us.

Background singers for "Good Ride Cowboy"

JERROD NIEMANN: We weren't coming up with a lot, just talking details, little things that could go in there, and this went for a few hours. Garth is kind of just listening. He's not writing anything down, so we don't know exactly what he's thinking. Then, after those two hours, he picks up a guitar, has a verse and a chorus done. Everything we'd talked about, he'd turned into a song! In his head! This is superstar shit here. Just an unbelievable songwriter.

RICHIE BROWN: The next time we heard anything about it, after working on it in Oklahoma, was sitting in chairs at Garth's studio. Garth was like, "Get ready, guys, because here it goes." Here came that B3 organ, and I got to hear "Good Ride Cowboy" for the first time.

BRYAN KENNEDY: This song, at its heart, was Garth's tribute to his hero. It's a shame Garth's name isn't on it. He said it was enough for him that he got to sing it.

MILTON SLEDGE: "Good Ride Cowboy," that was just a good ole country shuffle. At that time, I lived in Mount Juliet, Tennessee, and that's where Chris LeDoux lived. He was a guy known for selling cassettes out of the trunk of his car, at least back then, all the while following rodeo shows. He became a phenomenon, unbeknownst to me at the time. But obviously Garth, with the cowboy thing and the rodeo mindset, was definitely in tune with him. If you'd ever seen a Chris LeDoux show, you could immediately see the parallel between that and a Garth Brooks show.

CHRIS LEUZINGER: We worked on it quite a bit before we got this song right. Lots of walk-ups and walk-downs we did together, which always sounded so cool. But this is a good example of how Garth always wanted Rob, Bruce, and me to not be too polite about it all, you know, getting out of each other's way. He wanted us to play like it was late night in a bar, and we were all just going for it.

WE WERE ALL JUST GOING FOR IT.

—Chris Leuzinger

ROB HAJACOS: I couldn't give them enough of that crazy vibrato, that arrogant, slam-it-in-your-face fiddle. The order of the day was kind of, "Play until we tell you not to."

BRUCE BOUTON: "Good Ride Cowboy" was kind of a fun, rambunctious song. Garth wanted to turn us loose.

G: That's the G-Men at their best right there. And then we did the same thing that we did with "Friends in Low Places," just got fifty people in here, all singing that "Just LeDoux it!" That was a fun, fun line for that. Chris's guys came over. TK, all of them. They listened before they sang on it, and we all sat in the control booth and cried. It was good, a kind of a cleansing. Then they got out there, got to party and sing. I hope that's the way Chris would've wanted it.

Opposite: God bless Chris LeDoux…

IT WAS GOOD,
A KIND OF
CLEANSING. –g

ALLISON MIRANDA

By BOBBY WOOD, DAN ROBERTS & GARTH BROOKS

G: Allison Miranda is a twin. She was in the fan club. I just saw her and her sister down in Florida. She was part of that fan club that would house you when you couldn't afford to find a place to sleep, bring food to you when you couldn't afford to feed yourself. They were in it from the word go. And they were awesome. I always told her, I said, "Your name, Allison Miranda, should be a song. It just rolls off." And she said, "Yeah, yeah, yeah."

MARK MILLER: Bobby Wood and Garth would come in and write sometimes. And it seemed like they'd always find something. Bobby's a great writer…and a fair piano player. (laughs)

DAN ROBERTS: It was really interesting the way that song got written. It's Bobby Wood, Garth, and myself. Garth and I were writing together around that time, I think on another title. But he played me the chorus of that song, "I used to think of autumn / as sweaters and leaves." He played me that and told me what he was trying to do. Bobby Wood's a legend, plays all that amazing piano on Garth's records. Bobby and I are friends, and we were writing some stuff together anyway, so Garth said why don't I meet with Bobby and see if we can get this further down the road. So, Bobby and I got together and wrote on it, maybe got a little further, and then we gave Garth what we'd written.

BOBBY WOOD: Was this a ghost or was it real? The girl that he picked up on the road, I can't remember. Somewhere

YOUR NAME SHOULD **BE A SONG.** —g

along the line, me and Dan Roberts were going to make Allison Miranda a ghost. If I'm not mistaken, I think me and Garth had the melody part of the writing done, but the story wasn't finished.

NO TWO SONGS
ARE WRITTEN THE SAME WAY.

—**Dan Roberts**

DAN ROBERTS: At first, we had this guy driving, and he picks up a girl, a hitchhiker. He's tired, and she asks him won't he please pull over. So, he does, sleeps in his cab, and when he wakes up the next morning, there's a kiss on the rearview mirror, a lipstick trace, and she's gone. He pulls back out on the highway, drives around the corner, and in the light of day he finds that the bridge had washed out. So, she was more of, you know, almost an angel. But then it changed, as songs do in most cases. That's part of what I love about the songwriting

process: finding them. No two songs are written the same way. We gave Garth what we had, and he took it from there. But I don't remember hearing anything else about it after that. That was '98 or '99.

G: "I used to think of autumn / as sweaters and leaves / I used to think the night was just / for dreamers and thieves." That's when you step back and go, "Forgive me. Forgive me. But that's a great line right there." You might have had something to do with it, so that's why you ask for forgiveness, to boast about it. But it's just so right. Until she came into his life, that's what he saw. Then after meeting the one, all he saw during the fall, and all he saw during the night, was her. Beautiful.

DAN ROBERTS: Garth basically finished it the way that he heard it and saw it going. Then, years later, I get a call, find out I've got this song on *The Lost Sessions*, which was so cool. That came out of nowhere. I'd been down in Texas, hadn't seen Garth for three or four years. That was a real gift. Another gift from Garth.

G: I remember the day I saw Miss Allison, it might have been at spring training down in Florida. I said, "It's done. There's a song with your name, 'Allison Miranda.'" She goes, "You're full of shit." I said, "There is." First it was on a Ty England record. But I loved it so much I wanted to do my own version. And, man, the thing I love about this again is Milton Sledge. Milton Sledge laid a groove down on this thing that was rock solid. And then here comes Flux again, Jerry Douglas on dobro, and he plays all the coolest and most tasteful stuff. He took that song over. Just great guys. I think Sam Bush is playing on this record, as well. And when you put those guys on a recording, they create a groove that's so frickin' deep, you can't get out of it. *Love* this record, and what I love about it is it's very early '80s Garth in college. This song takes me right back there.

...MAJESTIC. -g

LOVE WILL ALWAYS WIN

the duet with Trisha Yearwood

By GORDON KENNEDY & WAYNE KIRKPATRICK

GORDON KENNEDY: That was written in that period of time when Wayne Kirkpatrick and I would call each other saying, "Let's get together and write and see what happens." You spend years as a songwriter trying to figure out how to get a song to a particular artist, generally not knowing exactly how or managing to pull it off. Then we wrote "Change the World" with Tommy Sims, which Wynonna Judd cut. And then Eric Clapton recorded it, got a Grammy, and things were different for us. After something like that happens, people like Bonnie Raitt call you and go, "Will you guys write me a song?" "Love Will Always Win" was written before that, when we got together to write, just seeing what might happen. Sometimes it took a while before a song found a home, if it did at all. And that song had a long, long road before it got in Garth's hands. But we sure were happy when it did.

G: "Love Will Always Win," this is the *Braveheart* of songs. Of romantic songs. This is the shield and the sword. And this is going to battle. Risking your life and everything for love. *But the world will bend / and the fight will end / Love will always win.* Wow. Pretty majestic.

WAYNE KIRKPATRICK: That song had such a long journey to get to the point of coming out on *The Lost Sessions*. Me and

Gordon had written that song several years back, and I believe we wrote the song for a movie initially, but nothing came of it.

G: I do know that we had "Love Will Always Win" ready for *Scarecrow*. It came down to that or "Squeeze Me In." Allen Reynolds said, "I think we have the Trisha and Garth ballads. Let's do something upbeat and fun." So "Squeeze Me In" edged it out. By the time of *The Lost Sessions*, "Love Will Always Win" had been around us for a while.

GORDON KENNEDY: Garth and Trisha, those two are cut of the same cloth, from their humor to the way they see the world to the

WE DIDN'T SEE THIS AS A DUET WHEN WE WROTE IT.

—Gordon Kennedy

way they treat the people around them. We didn't originally see this as a duet when we wrote it, but it made so much sense when I heard it that way, with those two people in particular.

TRISHA YEARWOOD: You know, we never did a duet that we didn't cut with the two of us singing live in the same room, typically with the band. There's something special that happens that you'll never get any other way. But a lot of times singers aren't in the same room when they sing a duet. That sounds crazy, but it's true. Because it's easier for the engineer to fix things if you're all separated. But Garth always believed there was such an energy in doing it together, and if one of us needed to go again, we could both just go again. And it just created that buzz, that feeling. It's a true performance. And this one felt like a big song. It needed us together. And we were.

G: "Love Will Always Win," you have to remember, at the time *The Lost Sessions* was being put together, this was like our theme song. That's where we're at in our life together. You're going to have to go to war. You're going to lose friends *because* you're together. You're going to make new friends *because* you're together. You're going to disrupt a way of life *because* you're together. Then you'll create a new one *because* you're together. So, the whole question is, are you going to do what it takes? Do you believe enough in this love? Because we don't like change, we just don't. But, again, you look to your side, and there she is. And you feel her hand in yours. Bring it. B*ecause the world will bend / and the fight will end / Love will always win.*

IT NEEDED US TOGETHER.

—Trisha Yearwood

SHE DON'T CARE ABOUT ME

By BRUCE ROBISON

G: In a music city, like a Tulsa or an Austin, you're going to have two kinds of writers. There are going to be the folks that can write the commercial stuff, and there are going to be these other guys that are really cool but their stuff's just never going to be commercial. Bruce Robison and his brother Charlie seem to walk a line right there in the middle. They seem to be able to come up with commercial stuff and still be cool. That's a gift all of us want.

BRUCE ROBISON: Garth, he's just—I'm sure you hear this all the time—he's just the most affable dude you'll ever meet. I was in the studio when he cut this song as producer for Ty England. When I was leaving, I picked up this old Takamine guitar and started out of the studio. Garth was like, "Oh, excuse me, Bruce, pardon me." He pointed down, and he was like, "You have my guitar." And I had this guitar that he's played forever, kind of legendary instrument. I grabbed it instead of my guitar as I was walking out. He was just kind to a fault, you know?

G: Ty's record is the only thing I've ever done as a producer. But what I did in that role is I cut songs with the artist that I'd want to cut myself. It's fun to get to do that. "She Don't Care About Me," well, Ty and I were living together in the trailer. Sandy and I were in a kind of trial

Garth with Ty England

separation. On the farm there was a house, but there was also this thing we called "the trailer." It was a double-wide, unbelievable, probably one of the nicest things I've ever lived in in my

101

IT GIVES YOU **CONFIDENCE AS A WRITER.**
—Bruce Robison

life. We'd call it the trailer more out of fun than anything. It was immaculate, huge, a blast, and an instant home. Ty lived on one side of it; I lived on the other. Every morning, man, I'd wake him up with "She Don't Care About Me." Just playing it over and over.

TY ENGLAND: There are different kinds of producers out there, but Garth is definitely on the fun side of things. And when he gets hooked on a song, he's gonna make sure you hear it.

BRUCE ROBISON: Ty cut two of my songs on the record he recorded with Garth, and that was a really big deal to me. The other one was "Travelin' Soldier," which The Chicks did later. When I hear that somebody kind of likes my stuff, it's just such a big deal, you know, finding out you're on somebody like Garth's radar screen. Like, *"He what?!"* It gives you some kind of confidence as a writer that you can't get any other way.

G: The Skinner Brothers is where we started, there in Stillwater, Oklahoma. That feel on "She Don't Care About Me" was Craig Skinner's bass line. It just sounded like it came right out of Stillwater, Oklahoma. And that's where Ty and I went to school. So, this song was a place where we felt very much at home. That groove was an easy, kind of fun thing to cut.

BRUCE ROBISON: It's a complete groove thing, that's all it is. The lyric is not William Faulkner or anything. But I think they liked the feel on the demo, so they called me in for the session with Ty. I guess they were hoping to get some grease on there, and I was glad that they gave it a shot with me. I'm not even in the top 10,000 acoustic guitar players in Nashville, but they had me play acoustic guitar and sing harmony at the same time, which I've never done before or since. It was like, there's no rules here with this guy Garth. He's going to try anything. And I went along with putting the guitar and vocal down at the same time, and

I guess it worked. So that was the first time I met him. Then, later, I learned that he cut "She Don't Care About Me" himself.

G: It was one of those songs that just stayed with me. We cut Ty's version, which I loved, but this song wasn't done with me. I just had to cut my own version. Bruce is just a fabulous writer. Same with his brother.

BRUCE ROBISON: So, he cut it, but then it went for years. From the time we knew Garth did it to when it came out was a long stretch, and Garth had retired, which meant that we'd kind of figured it might not come out at all. When I heard it, though, it was groovy, just right. They had this shit down. I've had a couple of songs cut that I would have said, "Well, these are the last ones that anybody would want to record." And that's one of them, you know? So, this was really, really cool. You never know what the life of a song is going to be. "She Don't Care About Me" has had a good life. Garth gave it that.

THAT GIRL IS A COWBOY

By JERROD LEE NIEMANN, RICHIE BROWN & GARTH BROOKS

G: A guy pulled me over at a breakfast place. He goes, "See that little girl over there?" And he points at this little shit-kicker, looks like she's about seven. She had her jeans tucked in her boots and wearing a beat-to-hell cowboy hat. She was sitting there eating breakfast, just piling it in. Little skinny, tough thing. He goes, "'That Girl Is a Cowboy.' That's me and hers song right there. That one's ours."

> ## THAT'S ME AND HERS SONG, RIGHT THERE.
> # THAT ONE'S OURS. –g

TRISHA YEARWOOD: Well, it's Tami Rose. That's who Garth had in mind. This song, to me, is about how all women kind of want to feel like guys think they're strong. I know the highest compliment you can pay me is to make me feel like I'm as tough as a guy but I'm still a woman. I think that's what this song is about. It's about paying the ultimate compliment to a woman like myself. Not saying, "You're so cool, you're almost like a guy." That's not what the song is saying. I think it's saying, "Man,

she's tough. That's a real woman there." I love that song.

G: For me, yeah, this song started with Tami Rose. Here's the story: We had two horses, Crackerjack and Little John. The reason why these horses mean so much to me, they're the first horses I ever got to own by myself. Because we could finally afford horses. Crackerjack was my horse. He was a paint, beautiful, a gaited saddle pony. It was like sitting in a La-Z-Boy. An old man, he would trip over his own shadow. But he took great care of me. We had been on each other's backs several times in the five years that we were together. Which means we took a lot of falls together. He'd roll over on me, he'd come up, and I was on his back all the time.

BRYAN KENNEDY: Garth's dressing room has some celery, broccoli, carrots, and some bottled water. I think if he probably wasn't married, he'd be in a house like the cowboy house in Oklahoma, the little yellow house. I remember going to him around 1992, after he'd picked up a lot of platinum records, and

THAT GIRL
IS A
COWBOY

THAT'S A **REAL WOMAN** THERE.

—Trisha Yearwood

L to R: Garth, Tami Rose, Richie Brown, and Jerrod Niemann

saying, "You need to get you a horse." He just wasn't much for getting anything for himself. So, he got a horse. That was Crackerjack.

G: It was the last horse my mom ever rode, and the first horse my oldest daughter ever rode. Cracker was as much a part of our lives as any dog you ever had. It was Tami who found him lying in the field. We had just moved back to Oklahoma and didn't have a place to keep them yet. She found him in the evening and called me from Nashville. I said, "Tami, I can't get there until tomorrow." She goes, "What do I do?" I said, "I don't think you can do any-thing. But I'll get there as soon as I can." When I get out into the field the next morning, I see it. There's Tami, what's left of a campfire, she's lying right next to Crackerjack. With a 30/30. She'd kept the coyotes off of him all night.

BRYAN KENNEDY: That's an image that'll stay with you for a long time.

G: Bob Doyle had been suggesting I write with some writers I didn't know. Just about that time was when I met Richie Brown. Good guy from

Texas. Richie told me about his friend Jerrod Neimann, who he writes with. I said, "Send me what you two have got."

JERROD NIEMANN: We recorded like fifteen songs, on something like a jam box, and dropped 'em off the next day.

RICHIE BROWN: We sent Garth all kinds of stuff. And we couldn't believe it—he called us back. He said, "I didn't hear anything that I necessarily wanted to cut from those CDs you sent." I said, "Oh, that's okay." Then he said, "But what I did hear was a couple guys who kind of come from where I'm from. And I'd really just like to get together with you." I about had a heart attack! Then he called Jerrod.

JERROD NIEMANN: I'm working at Chili's, waiting tables. I'm actually taking someone's order when I get a call from a private number. I gotta take it. The people I'm waiting on are looking at me like, what? It's Garth. I have Garth Brooks on the phone, telling me to come out that next Sunday. I can't believe this. I get off the phone, apologize, say, "That was Garth

Brooks." The guy looks at me and says, "I don't care if that was Jesus Christ. I'm hungry."

G: They came to the house, the big house in Nashville. This was before we wrote "Good Ride Cowboy." We're in the kitchen. I pull up one of the kitchen chairs, ask them what they want to write. Richie goes, "I just want to write one of those Garth Brooks things, man." I had that image of Tami with Crackerjack in my mind. "That Girl Is a Cowboy." How about that?

JERROD NIEMANN: I'm thinking, "What the hell does that mean?" Then he told us the story.

BOB DOYLE: There's so much range to Garth Brooks songs. He's always kept pushing on the possibilities. There's a lot he can do. And he can write from so many points of view.

RICHIE BROWN: It was like something out of a movie. Boom! "It was a 107 / we were heading to town / She had her sleeves rolled up / and the windows rolled down." I'm sitting there with my jaw open.

JERROD NEIMANN: "Hell, yeah!"

G: I think George Strait would have kicked the shit out of this song. That's kind of what you want to feel every time you sit down to write anyway. You want to feel like, "Man, if the King would sing this, it would be awesome!" But Strait could sing the phone book and I'd love it.

RICHIE BROWN: We didn't finish it. But you're just excited, like, "Oh, my gosh, we have a chance to make it on *Scarecrow*!" Then it didn't happen. So, for five years I'm walking around Nashville, telling publishers I got to write with Garth Brooks. People just slammed the door in my face, because they're like, "Well, he didn't cut it, so who cares?" But I feel like

Garth's a timing guy. Something like "Long Neck Bottle" sat on the shelf for, what, nine years? If the timing wasn't right for us with *Scarecrow*, it might be just right on another.

G: Its moment came. I invited them to come out to Oklahoma.

RICHIE BROWN: It was a little bit of a culture shock. He just lived like we do! He woke up and took his kids to school, and when he got back, we went to work on the song.

STRAIT COULD SING THE PHONE BOOK AND I'D LOVE IT. –g

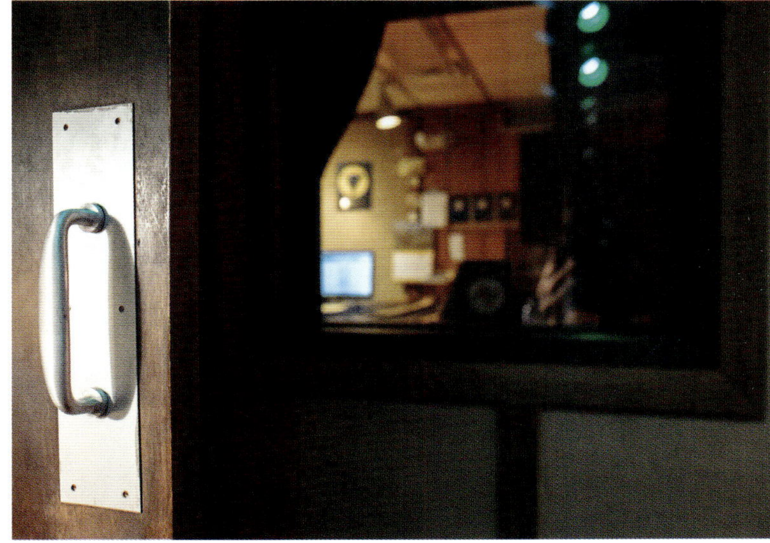

JERROD NIEMANN: What I found is that Garth is even cooler on the other side of the curtain. You know? The grace and kindness. I've learned a lot just watching how he moves through the world.

RICHIE BROWN: I still remember what Garth wanted for the sound of the recording because I've got a work tape of the song from back in the day. Garth was singing that twin fiddle part so that he would remember that it's going to have twin fiddles. Years later, the tempo has changed, but he still knew the fiddle part.

G: Rob Hajacos played twin fiddles on the recording. So good. That's a sound that'll always have a place in what we do.

ROB HAJACOS: My dad was a fiddle player, so I grew up hearing Ray Price's music, George Jones's. That's where I get my country influence. When I started playing fiddle in seventh grade, it was the first year that they offered orchestra in junior high school. So, I played Beethoven and Bach five days of the week, and then a couple nights a week I'd go play twin fiddles in joints with my dad.

MARK MILLER: Interestingly enough, we cut "That Girl Is a Cowboy" and "Good Ride Cowboy" on the same day. That was like a cowboy day, I would say. A good day.

FISHIN' IN THE DARK

By WENDY WALDMAN & JIM PHOTOGLO

VICTORIA SHAW: I love that he put "Fishin' in the Dark" on *The Lost Sessions*. That's like a country anthem. It's the perfect country song. One of my dearest friends, Jim Photoglo, wrote that with Wendy Waldman. The fact that Garth did this just tells me Garth was a superfan of it, as we all are. I got a kick out of that.

L to R: Jimmy Ibbotson, Jeff Hanna, Wendy Waldman, and Jim Photoglo

G: Jim Photoglo's a good dude. Wendy Waldman's a great dude, too. I love her. She's the one that produced the New Grass Revival records. To get to work with these people who laid the road map out? It was great. This is one of those songs you just love to death. And though I had no idea at the time, what this song would become for us *live* would be a whole other story.

WHAT THIS SONG WOULD BECOME FOR US *LIVE* WOULD BE A WHOLE OTHER STORY. —g

JIM PHOTOGLO: Well, I met Wendy at a wedding of a mutual friend in Los Angeles. She had a very powerful presence. In those days, she was very colorful in her attire. Bigger than life. She said, "Hi, I'm Wendy Waldman." And I said, "Well, I've heard of you." By the end of the conversation, we had exchanged phone numbers. The next day I got a call from a guy in the Commodores saying they were looking for songs. So, I called her up and I said, "Hey, let's write." She was just getting ready to move to Nashville. Now, understand, she's second generation. Her father wrote the theme songs to *Perry Mason* and *The Bullwinkle Show*. He scored movies. And Wendy's *high school* band was Bryndle, which included Andrew Gold, Karla Bonoff, and Kenny Edwards.

MILTON SLEDGE: One thing that stands out for me on *The Lost Sessions* is "Fishin' in the Dark." Mike Chapman and myself had played on the original demo for Wendy Waldman and Jim Photoglo. That was the demo that got them a cut with the Nitty Gritty Dirt Band. And it had ridden the charts, been a big hit. So, when Garth says, "Hey, I want to do this song," we go, "Cool! Full circle!"

JIM PHOTOGLO: Wendy talked me into coming to visit her in Nashville. The energy here just completely arrested me. So, I moved to Nashville. Wendy was my primary co-writing partner, and we tore it up. I'd left Los Angeles on my knees, and this place just saved my life. And she's a principal part of that. So, she's my

sister, and that's how I think of her. We're very close.

G: I was in my twenties when I first heard "Fishin' in the Dark." It was around the same time they had "Long Hard Road" out. My God, the Nitty Gritty Dirt Band. I'm a folk and bluegrass guy, so I love this. Everybody knew them as more of a pop kind of thing in the '70s. But they never were pop. I mean, "Mr. Bojangles" was popular, but not pop. But when Nitty Gritty Dirt Band all of a sudden reappeared on country radio in the '80s, I'm doing the solo sets at Willies. This is right down my alley. I'm playing everything they've got.

TRISHA YEARWOOD: I love the Nitty Gritty Dirt Band. When I say this, I want to make sure that it gets printed. I love the Nitty Gritty Dirt Band!

JIM PHOTOGLO: Before I bought a place in Nashville, I was staying at Shoney's on Demonbreun. I'd been tuning my guitar down a whole step. Wendy had just finished listening to *Prairie Home Companion.* She said, "Let's write a song about fishing." And I looked at her and thought, *what?* I wanted to run away screaming. She goes, no, fishing in the dark. This was just a moment, a genuine product of inspiration, of just everything happening at the right moment in time and us catching something.

G: When "Fishin' in the Dark" came out, I just thought it was amazing. So, it was always something I wanted to cut. Our version came from a knocking-the-rust-off session in, like, '98 or '99, I think. We just did some covers. Allen and Mark were trying to help me shift from the road back to the studio. But it turned out so good that you just wanted to keep doing it.

I WANTED TO RUN AWAY SCREAMING.

—Jim Photoglo

MARK MILLER: Allen was encouraging Garth to come in and play, just to do some of his favorite songs that he'd listened to on other people's records. Something fun can come out when there's no pressure. Garth was really busy, hitting the road hard, and this was a way to get into the studio rhythm.

TRISHA YEARWOOD: I don't know how Garth does this. It's happened with other things he's covered. I never thought I'd want to hear anybody but the Nitty Gritty Dirt Band sing this song. I loved their version so, so much. And then, after I heard Garth's version, and now having heard it live in years since, that's the version I want. I'm like, "How do you do that? How do you take a song that is so iconic that everybody knows because of this other artist and make it yours…make me love it even more?" If he would've asked me ahead of time, "Hey, I'm thinking about cutting 'Fishin' in the Dark.' What do you think?" I probably would've said, "No. You can't do that. That's Nitty Gritty Dirt Band." Yet he does it and makes it his, which speaks to the fact that he knows what's best for him.

MARK MILLER: "Fishin' in the Dark" was cut in 2000. And I'll have you know, I recorded the crickets on that track at my house. I had real good stereo separation. Got these great crickets. I've been paying them off ever since. (laughs)

FOR A MINUTE THERE

By KENT BLAZY & GARTH BROOKS

G: My dad was just one of those guys that… well, once Mom passed away, he just kind of stayed at the house. His place, his farm, still looked fabulous, of course, because that was his joy. He was a man who got up early and went to work. That's kind of the only thing he had after she died. They say a man does one of two things after losing the wife: he either gets remarried quickly, or he turns the house into a shrine. When my dad passed away ten years, maybe eleven years, after she did, her lipstick was in the same place she'd put it when she lived there. On her side of the bed. He would dust all around it. The pictures of her in the house, every picture, if the sun hit it just right, you'd see his lip prints on them.

IT WAS A WHOLE DIFFERENT TWIST FROM WHAT I'D THOUGHT OF.

—Kent Blazy

KENT BLAZY: It was hard for Garth to watch his dad's suffering after his mom died. His dad just wouldn't go on with his life after losing her. We actually kicked around a couple ideas about that, but we'd never done anything with them. Then this one came. And it really gets to the heart of what's going on when somebody passes away, leaving their partner among the living. I might start crying thinking about this, but for me, it started like this: my dad had passed away, and one day I was driving home from somewhere, and I saw this kid playing ball with his dad. That's what we used to do all the time. So, I came home and started writing this song, "For a Minute There." I sent what I had to Garth, and he calls me up and says, "I love this idea, but I'd like to work in something about my dad after my mom died." That gave it more direction, a whole different twist from what I'd thought of.

G: When dad would go to lunch somewhere, and you'd be sitting with him, my dad would lay out his wallet opened up to the pictures of her. He'd have lunch with her, while you ate with him. He also had this thing where he carried a framed picture of her wherever he'd go. If you'd have him come to the house, on the rare times he'd leave his own house, here he'd come with a suitcase and this picture underneath his left arm. He was a very athletic guy, had this powerful left arm holding this framed picture. He did it so much that when he didn't have the picture, his arm was in that position. It was tough to watch. But for me, it was always like going to school, just to watch it. It was learning about loss and how people live with it.

KENT BLAZY: I went to see Garth in Oklahoma with Kim Williams a few times, just to write. Then I went out there one time by myself because Garth wanted me to come out and work on "For a Minute There." We wrestled and wrestled with this thing, and couldn't really get it right. On my last night, I went back to the houseboat, and I just stayed up all night working on this thing, because I knew I was leaving the next day. I didn't know when I'd see Garth again. I thought maybe we needed to turn the verses around from where they were, make it almost surreal, you know, she's "standing ten miles out at sea." When we took it there, the song started to fall into place. I played it for Garth the next morning, and he liked what I'd done. Then we were able to get it finished.

IT WAS **TOUGH TO WATCH.** —g

G: We'd started this, God, I don't know how many years before. But it's just good, man. And a good thing never dies. It was one of those things where you said to yourself, "Okay, we've kind of got a start on it, but we're going to have to do something to get it done." Some come easy, some take time.

KENT BLAZY: I love where Garth took it from my first version, you know? He'd made it where anybody could identify with it, which is what he's so great at. Then having Alison Krauss on it, I mean, that's phenomenal to me. I knew it had been cut, but I didn't know Alison Krauss was singing the harmony on it or anything like that. So, once he calls up and says, you know, I want it to be on this *Lost Sessions* record, and Alison Krauss is on it, I'm like, "Okay, another gift I wasn't expecting."

G: Alison Krauss was one of my dad's favorite singers. And here she was on a song that was written for my dad about my mom. It was a lot of fun, and it was also very emotional, very healing, whatever you want to call it. For me *and* my dad, it came at a good time.

I'D RATHER HAVE NOTHING

By MIKE MCCLURE

MIKE MCCLURE: I grew up in a little town an hour from Stillwater, which was the first town I moved to that was bigger and, like any college town, had a variety of people coming in. It wasn't just the hundred people I grew up with. I got to meet real songwriters and the people that lived at a place called The Farm. Some of them were Garth's old band guys. It was the first place where I said, "Okay, I'm a songwriter, how do I do this?"

G: Mike McClure is the writer on this one. Mike was in this group called The Great Divide. Scotte, Kelley, JJ, Mike. Stillwater guys. Great guys.

I'M A SONGWRITER, HOW DO I DO THIS?
—**Mike McClure**

The Great Divide

MIKE MCCLURE: Some time after I moved to Stillwater in 1990, I was just sitting on my porch one day playing my acoustic, and a neighbor said, "Hey, I know a band looking for a guitar player." He takes me to meet these cowboys, and I played guitar with them. It really wasn't what I wanted to do, though, so I left that. I started writing, and in the first three songs that I wrote, there was "I'd Rather Have Nothing." I called one of the guys in that band and said, "Hey, would you come play drums on a demo?" We recorded three songs. That tape cassette kind of made its way around town. So, we felt like we needed a band to support this,

and that's when we all got together without their other singer and formed what became The Great Divide.

G: They were a Stillwater band with an Austin kind of feel. I knew Scotte Lester from bouncing out at the Tumbleweed. Scotte was just one of those regulars that would come in, a great guy, never got too drunk, real cowboy, would always help you out if you needed it. JJ was his younger brother. They're just horse guys, sweet guys. Mike McClure had this song called "I'd Rather Have Nothing." The line was, "I'd rather have nothing / than a whole lot of something I don't need."

MIKE MCCLURE: Grunge had come along and killed off the '80s rock that I was into in high school. Nirvana and all that was just a little too angry for me. Then Garth came out, and I thought, man, this kind of reminds me of old country, like Merle Haggard. I think Garth did that for a lot of people. I think the world needed what he had to offer.

NEVER GOT TOO DRUNK, REAL COWBOY. —g

CHRIS LEUZINGER: Mike McClure is from Oklahoma, played in The Great Divide. I actually worked with them, ended up producing a record on them. Small world stuff. Great guys. Knowing Mike, this lyric is just so him. Kind of happy-go-lucky and just a little bit down and out. When we cut this with Garth, I didn't know Mike, met him later. Then I understood that the song is pretty authentic to him.

THIS SONG *IS* SUMMER. –g

G: I just loved the song. "I believe schedules are / one of life's worst infections." That's a great line. It makes you want to take your truck out on the highway and roll your windows down. Just feel that air come in, with that shitty radio at full volume, cranked so loud that it's crapping out on you, and you're just singing at the top of your lungs. That's what that song is to me. This song is summer.

MIKE MCCLURE: I first saw the name Port Aransas on my older brother's T-shirt. He'd gone down there on some spring break. So, I had that town lodged in my memory. Then I got down there myself, slept on the beach like a moron. With this song, I was just hoping I was writing something that people liked, which sounds kind of silly to say out loud. I was around twenty or twenty-one when I wrote that, listening to a lot of Jimmy Buffett. I was just swept up in that whole thing of being young and drunk and on an island in your mind.

G: I showed Mike and the others around Nashville when they came through. That's when I heard the song.

Scotte Lester

MIKE MCCLURE: When we recorded our first album, with Lloyd Maines down in Lubbock, we included that song. We were trying to figure out what to do next, and Scotte Lester said, "Hey, Garth sang at my wedding. I kind of know him." The only person Scotte knew was this superstar of country music. But then, wow, Garth invited us to his place in Nashville, sent his tour bus to pick us up. I'd never met anybody famous at this point. He was super cool. We wound up in the basement, listening to some songs that were going to be on *In Pieces*. He said, "Play me some of yours." So, I played him "I'd Rather Have

Garth, Randy Taylor, Allen Reynolds, and Mark Miller with The Great Divide

I WAS JUST CRUSHED,
TOTALLY CRUSHED.

—Mike McClure

Nothing." He said, "Play that song again, man." He had me play it like three or four more times, then asked me if he could cut it. "Hell, yeah."

G: We were lucky to build our foundation on albums. Because—c'mon, man—we can talk all day long about the singles, but it's the album cuts that save people's lives. Like this one. For some people, "I'd Rather Have Nothing" is going to be their song. Thank God you got Allen Reynolds. There's your base. When it came to putting albums together, sequencing them, Allen would do this thing where he'd write the name of each song out on a piece of paper, cut them out, then he'd carry this pile of song titles in his hand. At lunch, or standing and talking on the steps, he'd just be throwing those titles down and start arranging them. We thought a lot about where every song should be, no matter if it was going to be a single or not. We thought about the spaces in between them, how one felt going into another. Those album tracks meant everything.

MIKE MCCLURE: So, he cuts this song for *In Pieces*, and I go home and I just sit by the phone and wait. I mistakenly told all my friends what was going on. Then, several months later, Garth left me a voicemail that said, "Hey, man, I recorded this song for the album, but Allen Reynolds, the producer, doesn't really think it's right for this project. But I'd like to hang on to it." I was just crushed, totally crushed. Turns out I just had to wait for it and learn a bunch of lessons in between. One lesson was this: Don't tell anybody what you think is going to happen. I guarantee you, I learned that one.

G: When I produced Ty England's record, we cut it with him, had so much fun doing it.

MIKE MCCLURE: Having the biggest country act in the world saying, "Hey, I love your song and want to record it," it was just such a feather in my cap. Even if it didn't come to fruition at the time. But he produced an album for Ty England, had Ty cut that song. So, I went out to Nashville, got to sit with Garth, and he played Ty's version of "I'd Rather Have Nothing." It was kind of hard for me to go there and sit next to him, just me and him in the studio, blaring this track. It was kind of hard not to goon out, honestly. Just to see that song make the light of day and to hear how much time was put into it was so cool.

G: Doing it with Ty just confirmed yet again that this song was something I had a real connection to. So, when we were putting *The Lost*

IT CAN KEEP A SONGWRITER WRITING SONGS.

—Mike McClure

Sessions together, it came to mind right away. We put this one on the list, high on the list.

MIKE MCCLURE: After hearing Ty's version, I thought, "Well, that's probably the end of that." But Garth's true to whatever he says. He hung onto this song all those years. That meant more than I can tell you. In '05 I got the call that he was releasing *The Lost Sessions*, and that the song would be on it. Just being a part of this, what a thing for a songwriter, right? When I go to a room where I'm completely unknown, I can say that name, and they'll perk up and give you a little better listen. It can keep a songwriter writing songs.

ABC RECORDS
ALEXANDER HARVEY
EMI AMERICA STEREO
U.S.A.
SW-762
COLUMBIA STEREO
COLUMBIA STEREO
ST-11543
LION"
ANCHOR RECORDS
ANCL 2021
Printed in U.S.A.
R. MERCURY
RN NR 5001-LP
LOYD
EPIC STEREO
EPIC STEREO
BOOT RECORDS

COWGIRL'S SADDLE

By GARTH BROOKS, BRYAN KENNEDY & GARY MCMAHAN

G: So, Bryan Kennedy's out to visit, staying with me at the little yellow house there in Oklahoma. I'm on the phone with the guys from Walmart. We're writing a song…me and Bryan, that is.

BRYAN KENNEDY: Man, this is a great story. Garth was still working on the new house, so he was living in the little yellow place. You're kind of on top of each other in there. I went out to write with him, and we hadn't written in a while. At this point in time, he's on the phone a lot, and he's making some pretty big decisions to get the Walmart deal done. And, yeah, he's making some of those big decisions while we're in this writing session.

THIS IS A
GREAT STORY.

—Bryan Kennedy

G: It's as complicated a moment as I'd ever seen on the business side. All good guys with good intentions, just some miscommunication when the deal was translated to the "lawyer" side. And we're writing "Cowgirl's Saddle" while this "make it or break it" conversation is going on.

BRYAN KENNEDY: We had this story we'd seen somewhere, from an old poem or something, I'm not even sure. But it was so entertaining. A cowgirl's saddle: "It's between the two things you love the most." We had to write it.

G: In the song, the singer dies. God is talking. God asks him, "What did you love most in your past life?" / "Well, it had to be between cowgirls and horses" / And as I wondered which one I would settle on / God said, "May you

BRYAN KENNEDY: Something was happening along the lines of what got us in trouble with "Cowboy Cadillac." We got ourselves in a rhyme scheme jail again. It was "sew me, show me, throw me." There's all these internal rhymes. Once you start doing that, you have to follow through. And it's not as easy as it might seem from a distance. So, we're in that jail again. Really stuck, on this particular song.

G: Yeah, it's based off of a thing out of cowboy poetry, but what I loved was, "Okay, let's push

AND GOD SAYS, **"WATCH THIS."** –g

be happy with your answer" / I said, "What answer?" / And God says, "Watch this." And off this thing goes. I come back as a cowgirl's saddle. So, yeah, we're having fun writing this. There's no way not to.

BRYAN KENNEDY: But Garth's on the phone the whole time, wrestling with this business situation. (laughs)

G: It was like, "Hey, guys, we need to come back to center here." I wasn't even sure if, at this point, the deal with Walmart was going to happen or not. But I was in the middle of writing. I was having the time of my life, because I hadn't gotten to write songs in a while.

ourselves." It was, "Take me, break me, make me what you need." And Bryan's like, "Oh shit, are we really going to try and do this through the whole song?" I said, "Yeah. It'll be fun." But it was good. It was good, man. "Wrap me, slap me, strap me on your steed."

BRYAN KENNEDY: It had to have three rhyme words in there that were the right rhymes, every time it came around. It's a really daunting task. Finally, with nine lines done, we were right down to the end of this thing. Picture this: I'm sitting at his desk, I've got a pencil with an eraser that's totally gone because I've written and erased so many things. I'm frustrated that I'm not coming up with

anything. Garth is pacing back and forth, talking to somebody on the phone. He's all numbers and if-this-happens-then-that-will-happen, just in another world. I'm sitting there, trying to get this thing finished for when he's off the phone call. I'm straining to come up with the perfect ending while he's pacing and talking. This went on for maybe an hour.

G: The Walmart deal was a big deal, so it had to be right. There was some heavy lifting in there. But I wasn't going to miss a writing session with Bryan Kennedy. And, really, this wasn't the first time I'd done two things at once. Once you have kids, you better know how to change diapers and make a sandwich at the same time, and without getting them mixed up.

back to work on that deal, "Okay, so anyway, I was…" I freaked out.

G: I mean, this was a fun one to write. The song almost did the writing for us. Once that rhythm and rhyme get going, it's like a train. But, as writers, we won't forget that day. It'll live on for us. I love writing with this guy. It was a fun day, with one thing distracting you from the other. Every time you went back to the song, it was fresh.

I'VE NEVER BEEN SO PISSED OFF AT HIM IN MY ENTIRE LIFE.

—Bryan Kennedy

BRYAN KENNEDY: I'm trying my damnedest to get this last line done while he works. Then—I shit you not—he leans halfway through the door, his left shoulder on the door jamb, holds the phone to his chest to cover up the mouth part, and says, "How about 'Roping, loping, hoping that she's happy / Racing, placing, chasing all your dreams / Makes me think if I'd lived life a little better / Would I've come back as a pair of cowgirl jeans?'" And then he picks the phone up, puts it to his ear, and goes right

BRYAN KENNEDY: I'm like, "What?!" He'd just written the entire last verse while he's doing a business deal on the phone, no pen and paper. And not only did he write it, but it's freaking great. I've never been so pissed off at him in my entire life. You think you're doing a good job, and then somebody like him writes that? I'll tell you this: there is not a better songwriter than Garth Brooks. I'm not saying it because I'm trying to kiss his butt. I'm just telling you, he's that good.

UNDER THE TABLE

By GARTH BROOKS & RANDY TAYLOR

RANDY TAYLOR: Garth and I had a symbiotic relationship: he played in bars, and I hung out in them.

G: We go way back. Randy's as cowboy as it gets. So, as a writer, he really brings a lot of authenticity.

RANDY TAYLOR: Back in college, Garth and I had a mutual friend, Ted Larkin. Ted told me I should come see this guy who was playing

guitar down the street. I didn't care much for the place he was playing, Willie's, but I went because all my friends were going.

G: Of course, Randy's the guy who wrote "Much Too Young," one of the first people I ever wrote songs with.

RANDY TAYLOR: Most of the people I was listening to at the time were songwriters, what we call "red dirt" or "Americana" now, guys like Jerry Jeff Walker, Guy Clark, Willie Nelson. I always fancied myself to be someone working in that vein. I thought I was kind of philosophical, you know? So, after seeing Garth, I thought maybe we could write some songs. And I guess he could tolerate me enough to try it.

G: "Under the Table" is from the time of "Much Too Young." Everything with Randy was done early. After "Much Too Young" came out as our first single, Randy would come about once a year to Nashville to write. Mainly what we'd do is sit around and just talk about other people's songs, just having fun playing those. We wouldn't get much writing done, which is often true of songwriters. Randy wrote a song called "The Old Man's Back in Town" for us for a Christmas record. Great stuff. Stone country kind of stuff—that's what he does so well.

RANDY TAYLOR: First time I heard "Much Too Young," Garth was playing with his band. It was late, and there wasn't hardly anyone left in the place because it was closing time. They'd kind of run out of material. I don't think the band had played the song before, but they kind

Randy Taylor and Garth

NO OTHER SINGLE
WILL EVER FEEL LIKE YOUR
FIRST SINGLE FELT. —g

of just followed along. Garth had told me, "Hey, listen to this and tell me what you think." And the truth was, it was basically all there before I got involved. But right then it was more about being in the music industry than it was about rodeo. Garth came over after and asked me what I thought. I said, "It'd probably be better as a rodeo song." So, we scheduled a time to get together and work on it.

G: "Much Too Young" is a song that will always have a place in my heart. No single you put out will feel like your first single felt. You just don't forget that stuff. As songwriters, Randy and I shared that thrill.

RANDY TAYLOR: I was just finishing up my master's degree around the time Garth moved to Nashville. When his first record came out,

in '89, I'd moved into a faculty position at Kansas State University. Right about then, I got a call from Garth telling me that, well, "Much Too Young" might be on the album. Then as it got a little closer, he let me know that, yeah, it's going to be on there. Then, after the album was all recorded, he said, "I think this one might be the first release." I look back, and it's all just surreal. I guess it's hard for me not to see the guy who was in Stillwater. He's still the same guy— he just happens to live in Nashville and be one of the greatest recording artists of all time.

G: So, yeah, "Under the Table" is one we'd done early on. I think that song was the kind of thing that I loved more than I could do well, if that makes any sense. No matter how well you did it, all you could think of was how much better Haggard and Jones would have done it.

ALL YOU COULD THINK OF WAS **HOW MUCH BETTER HAGGARD AND JONES** WOULD HAVE DONE IT. —g

RANDY TAYLOR: Classic country stuff, that's what we were thinking about. Garth always comes back to the places he started from. It would be hard to find an artist in the last few decades who has done more cowboy songs than Garth Brooks. And then he's tackled some stuff that your average country artist wouldn't touch, like "We Shall Be Free." He pushes the limit on some things but also likes that play on words of classic country. Garth covers it all: humor, emotion, the big stuff, and the in-between stuff.

G: I've got a song called "Happy Anniversary, Darling (Wherever You Are)." It's that same stone country thing. We would do one or two or three of those for a record and very rarely would one of those three make it. It was just something in my past that still mattered to me. You've got to take a thousand swings at that stuff. Allen will sometimes tell me, "That's you." But occasionally he'll say, "Pal, that's you trying to be somebody else."

RANDY TAYLOR: Garth had always told me, "Some songs shouldn't be written." Like,

you might have a nice little idea, but that doesn't mean a song that should come of it. When he brought me "Under the Table," I said to him, "You know, some songs shouldn't be written." (laughs) But then it stuck with me. It was rattling around in my head. So, my wife and I were on vacation with some other couples, at Beaver Lake in Northwest Arkansas, and I called him on a pay phone. I left the first verse and chorus on his answering machine. Then he finished it, made a demo. I was in Nashville after that, and he played it for me. It was some other demo singer doing it, not Garth. This was the early '90s, so he was a busy guy. I loved it, but that was the last I heard of it.

G: I brought this idea to Randy because he is that guy. "The bartender just told me I had too much to drink / Now, why's he believing I give a damn what he thinks?" That's Randy Taylor. It was fun. Come time for *The Lost Sessions*, it was there in the vault, waiting.

RANDY TAYLOR: He never notified me about "Under the Table" coming out. I don't remember how I found out. I think I bought it and went, "Holy Crap! I got a song on here!" I had the CD long before the royalty checks rolled in! (laughs) But Garth never makes a big deal of himself. I'll tell you a story: I remember a time I was with him, it was a Friday night, and we were standing in line at Tumbleweeds, a dancehall here in town. He was going to play Willie's the next night. But we're waiting to get in, and there's two girls in front of us, and one of them is saying, "I was going to see Garth Brooks play tonight, but it was gonna be way too crowded." Garth just looked at me. That was it. It always stuck with me. He wasn't going to draw attention to himself, wasn't going to poke her and say, "Hey, I'm right here!" There just aren't too many people like that. I never forgot that moment. Tells you something about who he is. And who he is is who he's always been. Just not a fake bone in his body.

AMERICAN DREAM

By JENNY YATES & GARTH BROOKS

G: This was something Jenny Yates and I had started. It was pretty much all we had. For this project, we kind of wanted to leave it up to your imagination. Every child of my generation woke up every morning like this. Their dads would go off to work, and their dads would come home at five o'clock or six o'clock and play baseball with them in the backyard or do whatever. The next day, the same thing would happen. It was fun to kind of start this. There's a beautiful musical thing that just kind of allows each child of that generation to close their eyes and see their own dad and see their own life as a kid, living it again through this song.

JENNY YATES: "American Dream." Obviously, this title is massive. I continue to work on this song to this day. I believe it can be an even greater song, and I keep bringing it up to Garth and keep coming up with ways it

could go, as a lead-off to a great story. It's so relevant as we all question, look for, work for, and live the American Dream.

G: You got to remember that for me, a song is a song is a song. When they talk about "American Pie" being eight minutes and fifty seconds, well, a song can also be twenty-five seconds. James Taylor did that a couple times on his records,

I CONTINUE
TO WORK
ON THIS SONG
TO THIS DAY.

—**Jenny Yates**

L to R: Garth, Jenny Yates, and Trisha Yearwood

where the song just gets started and it stops. It's like something gets started, then it's handed over to the listener, and they finish it with whatever their story is. Jenny Yates was the one that taught me that twilight happens twice a day. I always thought it was only in the evening, but twilight also happens in the morning. She knows the subtleties. Jenny is the one that gives you a thousand ways to go. I just never found one with this song that felt like it should go there. It seemed to me like it shouldn't be any more than this. The song will tell you.

MARK MILLER: Jenny's been a really great co-writer with Garth. I haven't been around many writers that live it the way she does. She studies it and comes up with alternative lines, a million possible directions. I've been able to see it in her because we're friends.

JENNY YATES: Garth had an idea specific to him. I think his dad did some kind of work in the oil fields in Oklahoma. Maybe I brought in some of the anthemic ties to "The Star-Spangled Banner," I'm not sure. When I work with Garth, it feels like we're of one mind. When we're at our best, it's when we push each other—push for meaning, push for a better line, a better word. I like to call it whittling, continuing to carve away, finding the words that can be stronger and more specific. As Michelangelo said, "I saw the angel in the marble, and carved until I set

IT'S A **GREAT, NOBLE CALLING,** SONGWRITING.

—Jenny Yates

it free." All the ideas I've had the opportunity to work on with Garth have a great feel of zing and lift to them. They all have an angel or two in them. It's a great, noble calling, songwriting. And it's been great to get to work with an artist of such great talent and heart, and smarts. I so believe in Garth Brooks and his artistry, and all the good his music can do for people. I remain a fan.

G: What I love about "American Dream" is it's your story. No matter who you are. Your story is not going to look like my story, but it will play very well in the music bed that follows. The Captain, Dennis Burnside, did the string arrangements. He helped to create a musical place for people to go to think about their own lives, just like I was thinking about mine. My dad worked two jobs his whole life, but never, when I turned around to look up in the stands, never did I not find him at one of my games. Never was he not there for me after a hard loss. Always there. I don't know how he did it. You know, as a dad, it's hard not to focus on the times when maybe you weren't there. But I can't remember a time my dad wasn't there. Ever. My kids don't have that story. A man will blame having to make a living for the times he wasn't there for his family. We'll do that to justify why we're gone all the time. When you're on the road playing shows, there's sure no reading kids to sleep— that's right in the middle

THEY'RE YOUR REASON. —g

of the heart of everything. But I'm telling you, that reading kids to sleep thing, it's the best part about parenting. I could not do it from the road. I finally had to stand up and say I wasn't going to be a dad that saw my kids one weekend out of a month. I just wasn't going to be. Because my dad wasn't. You just had to say, "Hey, look, as much as I love doing music, being a parent is a thousand times better. No offense to music." Anybody that's ever been a parent knows there's nothing that beats that. I could live without music the rest of my life. I can't live without my children for one second. No parent can. They're your life and soul, your breath in, your breath out. They're your reason. This song "American Dream" tells you something about what was on my mind for so long.

I'LL BE THE WIND

By JOSH KEAR & MARK IRWIN

JOSH KEAR: It goes back to high school for me. I owned Garth's first records. I remember sitting around listening to Lon Helton interview him as *Ropin' the Wind* was being released. I was in my little bedroom in East Tennessee, recording each song on my tape deck as the commercials ended, just so that I could have the album a week before anyone else did. I'd written my first song at thirteen. I had a crush on a girl in my English class, and she had a crush on a guy in the sophomore English class. I didn't know how to process it. Without even thinking about it, I went home and wrote a song, and I literally have never figured out how to stop. When Garth's records started coming out, his stuff was right up my alley.

MARK IRWIN: I was tending bar at the Bluebird Café the night Garth did a showcase for some folks at Capitol Records. So, I was right there, watching from the beginning. You could really see there was something special about him. He had a higher quality of songs. I mean, I can remember his "Much Too Young," "If Tomorrow Never Comes," "Friends in Low Places." That first album, then *No Fences*, they're just full of great songs. Besides his skill as a performer, I think he has a true gift for writing, for picking a song, for working with the best co-writers. If you got a Garth cut, it really meant something.

G: Josh Kear and Mark Irwin are really good guys. I had this song on hold forever. We had cut it for *Scarecrow*, I think. I felt bad that it didn't make that record. Josh was a sweet kid. If I'd have known then that Josh was going to become the Elvis of songwriters, I wouldn't have worried about him. But this was one of his first holds. Now he's the guy. We knew we were going to get Martina McBride on it. Everything was going to rock. It just didn't work out. So, it went into the vault.

> # I WAS RIGHT THERE, WATCHING FROM THE BEGINNING.
>
> **—Mark Irwin**

Opposite: Martina McBride and Garth

JOSH KEAR: I've probably written more songs with Mark than anyone else on the planet. A guy named Jameson Clark connected us. We wrote a couple of truly horrible songs together at the very beginning. But we had a great time doing it, so we kept getting together. By our third or fourth song, we wrote one that made us kind of look at each other and go...something's happening. We'd finally gotten to the point where we'd stopped trying to write something commercial. We had that soul connection moment where we finally went, okay, we understand why we're sitting in a room together.

MARK IRWIN: It took a couple of attempts, but by the third or fourth time we wrote together, we really clicked. We've been the best of friends and consistent co-writers for twenty, twenty-five years now. "I'll Be the Wind" we kind of compared to "Running on Empty," at least that was the template in our heads. We're both huge Jackson Browne fans. Sometimes we'd sit there for hours, talking about music that we've loved. On that particular day, Jackson Browne was our inspiration. We have a couple songs in our catalog, you'd swear they were Eagles songs or Bruce Springsteen songs, just because of what we were talking about that day. We were just so into what we were doing.

JOSH KEAR: I'd read a book of Paul McCartney interviews, and he was talking about his writing sessions with John. They'd look at each other and go, "Who are we going to be today?" Then one of them would be like, "Let's be Little Richard." So, they'd sit around and write a song in the style of Little Richard. Then it would come out sounding like the two of them. Mark and I would do that same thing,

THE DEMO WAS
STRANGE…

—Josh Kear

Josh Kear

but we'd write a little mini album, where not every song had to sound like a single. "I'll Be the Wind" was one of five or six songs in the style of Jackson.

G: When I first heard the song, I thought of it as a beautiful soundtrack song for *Thelma and Louise*. Two women singing "I'll Be the Wind," you know? Like, "I'm your best friend, and I'm here for you." So, when it came to me cutting it, I'm thinking I need a female singing here. Martina McBride became this voice of the friend. It could have been your spouse or your mate. She opened it up to all kinds of different things, not just the romantic. I thought her performance on this was fabulous. I felt lucky to get to sing on her records, and now she was on our stuff.

JOSH KEAR: I got a call from my plugger, Michelle Berlin, the day after Thanksgiving. We all still had answering machines then. Apparently, Garth was sitting around listening to songs on the holiday, which didn't make a lot of sense to me. But I vividly remember that it was Thanksgiving. Nobody else had put the song on hold up to that point. The demo was strange, too, (laughs) because there's actually crowd noise mixed in through the whole thing. The band was having such a good time blowing through it, I turned around to my engineer and said, "Man, this sounds like a live record." As kind of a joke, he slid the crowd noise under the intro when I was out of the room. I was like, "Keep it! Put it behind the whole thing." He looked at me like I was insane.

"

MARK IRWIN: I think the applause was from a Billy Joel live record. It made our demo sound like a performance in front of a massive audience. We did some crazy stuff. But the song had such a good, live feel for a band.

MILTON SLEDGE: "I'll Be the Wind" is a cool song. It wasn't a single, but it was a well-thought-out, well-written song. I liked what Mike Chapman and I were able to create with that, just making that bed for the other guys to play on top of. Straightforward but with a little funk. Being from the Muscle Shoals area, that feel always crept into our playing, no matter what we were doing. It's in our musical DNA. This song let us go there.

MARK IRWIN: We were so excited to get a Garth cut, then we found out that "I'll Be the Wind" didn't make the album. Man, it was like a punch to the chest. Part of the business, but not an easy part.

JOSH KEAR: That was a tough day. But I have to say this: Within a week of finding out that our song hadn't made the Garth album, checks showed up. Garth, or someone from his camp, sent checks to each of us. The message wasn't "We're releasing this." It was "We're sorry we held up the song for so long and did not use it." I'd never heard of anyone doing this before or since. I felt like, wow, somebody over there understands songwriters and the struggles they go through, especially early in their careers. I used that money to buy the guitar that I've written most of my hit songs on. A 1967 D35 Martin. Garth bought it for me. He didn't know it, but he bought it for me, for a song that didn't make an album. It was crazy.

G: For *The Lost Sessions*, "I'll Be the Wind" was one of the ones that I looked at and went, "This has definitely got to be on the record." It had been so close to being on a record anyway.

MARK IRWIN: It was just a thrill for me to hear about the song getting on *The Lost Sessions*. Just to be part of anything attached to Garth. It even had Martina McBride on it, which

JUST MAKING THAT BED FOR THE OTHER GUYS TO PLAY ON TOP OF.

—Milton Sledge

made it that much more special. Garth's a real person, still just a dude from Oklahoma who wants to watch college football. He showed up at the Bluebird just last night. The show was Tony Arata, who wrote "The Dance," Pat Alger, Kent Blazy. All songwriters who have written for or with Garth, playing for 150 people. And Garth showed up, did the show with them. That's how real he is.

JOSH KEAR: I remember when I found out it would make *The Lost Sessions*—once again, I got a call from that same plugger, saying, "Hey, this is bizarre, but Garth's putting out a record of songs that got away, and your song's going to make the album." I was standing in a parking lot, and I screamed my head off. I knew that for the rest of my life I was going to be able to say, "I'm part of the Garth Brooks story."

MEET ME IN LOVE

By GARTH BROOKS, BRYAN KENNEDY & BOBBY WOOD

G: Me and Bryan Kennedy put the lyric together on this one. But it was Bobby Wood who brought the real soulful Memphis Boys kind of feel to it. So sweet. Bobby Wood has heard so much music in his life, to get any kind of response out of him is almost impossible. But when he heard that little falsetto thing I was singing, Bobby looked up and went, "Oh, that's nice." When he said that, it was like, "Well, maybe we have something here, and we should probably turn it over to Bobby!"

BRYAN KENNEDY: Garth got with Bobby Wood after we had a lot of the lines written. The verses were done, and the basic melody was there. But when it got to Bobby, that's when it became the song you hear on *The Lost Sessions*. Bobby is a legend, and for good reason.

BOBBY WOOD: I had a groove going on. And I believe Garth heard it and said, "Let's do that." It came straight out of R&B.

G: There's something about Bobby. A man of few words. But there's not a player in our sessions who doesn't sometimes look over at him and go, "That's fucking Bobby Wood. I'm playing with Bobby Wood." Everybody talks about him. He's a Hall of Fame shoe-in if they ever get around to those legendary players.

IT ISN'T HARD TO STAY HUMBLE IN A ROOM WHERE BOBBY WOOD IS AT THE PIANO. —g

There's some of them that need to go in, and he's one. It isn't hard to stay humble in a room where Bobby Wood is at the piano.

BRYAN KENNEDY: I really love this song. It's such a different thing, especially for me. Because it's not funny. It's not a rodeo cowboy or anything like that.

G: Yeah, man. It's all about…it's sex on a record. That's what I like about it. "The warmth of your body / your breath on my skin / your touch is ungodly / and way beyond sin." You put those lines back-to-back. Well, that's good stuff right there.

BRYAN KENNEDY: It's the moment when something triggers that feeling of "Oh, my gosh, this person is my person." It could be two people that have been dating for two years, and they have this sense, suddenly, that they're ready, they really see each other. The dance floor is empty, the moment comes, and the feelings line up. Theoretically, it could be about one of those moments in an individual's life. It could be you've broken up with somebody, you're single, but you're sitting there in the place where they're dancing. It's that elegance of a rela-tionship. Not the hookup or some one-nighter. To me, it was like an elegant way of saying forever. That's what I hope some-body hears in that song.

G: It's cool. And Bobby was a key to this, not just in the writing but in the recording. He winds and moves with the group. Bobby does two great things: One is to allow space. Bobby will tell you this, he can lay out with the best of them, just not play. The whole band will be playing. Bobby will be looking down at the keys. You push Bobby, but nothing is happening. Sometimes you even think he's playing. Bobby knows that there's points in a song when space is the best thing that he can give. The second thing he does is he'll stay on something if he knows it's right. As much as it might be against what everybody else in the band is doing, he'll stay on it. What happens then is that, one by one, each of these guys finds a way to bend, get back to where Bobby is. You've got a guy that knows when to lay out and a guy that knows when not to give up. There's the captain of your ship right there.

BRYAN KENNEDY: It started as an idea that I had, and I think I mentioned it to Garth. We might have been on horseback. I don't remember. But I loved the final recording. I was surprised to see it on *The Lost Sessions* because I didn't even know he'd recorded it. Garth sang his butt off on it. He can make you feel what-

> ## HE CAN MAKE YOU FEEL
> # WHATEVER IT IS
> ## HE WANTS
> # YOU TO FEEL.
>
> —Bryan Kennedy

ever it is he wants you to feel. He makes being a co-writer easy, makes me look real good. I'm always amazed at what comes out of that studio after they're done.

G: What you hear is the original piano/vocal demo when we wrote the song. We took that out of the vault and just added the other instru-ments to that original track. It's a fun song for me. I like putting on all the different costumes. You can be a hopeless romantic. You can be a dreamer. You can be an explorer. You can be a guy that's brokenhearted. You can do all that stuff in the music. That's amazing. When a chance like this comes up, where an over-weight white guy gets to be sexy, it's a fun role to get to play. (laughs)

YOU CAN'T HELP WHO YOU LOVE

By MARCUS HUMMON & STEVE WARINER

STEVE WARINER: Marcus Hummon, what a brilliant songwriter. We've written a lot of songs together, and he wrote a bunch of hits for The Chicks and so forth. But when we started working on a song called "You Can't Help Who You Love," I remember thinking maybe Garth would be interested and sending what we had over to him.

G: This was something Steve pitched. Marcus Hummon, sweet guy, great writer. And you're not going to find a better guy than Steve Wariner, as a man, as a writer and musician. I love him. When Steve reaches out, you'd be a fool not to respond. So, he sent "You Can't

Help Who You Love," and we tried it, just a little piece of it, but it wasn't working. So, this was one of those things, like "Long Neck Bottle," that stayed in the top drawer but never got to actually find a place on a record.

STEVE WARINER: Garth called me and said, "Man, I love the idea of this song." He goes, "I like where you're going with it, but I'm not seeing where it fits with my thing. I'm not seeing the connection for me." Now, I'll say this, and I think it's really important: What I love about Garth is that he looks at songs and judges them for whether they represent some truth in his world and his situation. To sing

them, to give himself to them completely, he needs that sense of connection. That's one reason he's such a great performer and singer—he's feeling this stuff as he's doing it. And we can tell. So, when he listens to a song, he's looking for that connection. When he tells you it's not working, this is kind of what he's talking about. So that's what I think was going on with this song. It just wasn't relating to where he was in his life at the time. It didn't fit in there.

HE LOOKS AT SONGS FOR HOW THEY REPRESENT SOME TRUTH IN HIS WORLD.

—Steve Wariner

G: So, the song is in the top drawer, but then one day around that same time, I'm hearing about this trial on the news. It was a big deal, lots of coverage. This convicted killer, a guy who took the lives of several people, really evil, is being tried. You just see this in his face. But every day as he walks into the courtroom, right behind him is his mother. Walked with this man every day. Cried for him every day. You can't help who you love. There it was. That was a big statement. And then the song made this kind of sense for me. I knew this story. Here it is.

STEVE WARINER: Garth calls me— and you could tell he was a little hesitant, saying, "You guys are already working on this thing, so I don't want to interfere"—but he says, "Maybe you could rework this thing?" This is the kind of moment when you start to get excited for a song. I call Marcus, and of course he's like, "Oh my God, that would be awesome." You kind of understood that something had given Garth a connection to the song.

ALLEN REYNOLDS: Garth is an emotional singer. He really gets inside of the song. He's a great singer in any case, but when he feels a connection to the material…that's when things start to happen.

STEVE WARINER: So, Garth got involved with us, and we hammered the song out and finished it. I love it that he caught onto that whole premise of, you know, *you can't help who you love*, the title. I remember going to his place, the place off of Concord Road. We spent the evening working on it. I took my acoustic, and we sat around, we ate, hung out, and…that's songwriting, right?

G: You might be playing basketball, you might be taking a walk, you might be sharing a meal. And on a good day, you're songwriting the whole time.

STEVE WARINER: To me, Garth's sensibilities are that he's really a writer. That's the heart of the matter. He's a sensitive, emotional writer. The real deal. That's what comes first when you think about what makes this guy who he is. He won't give up on it until every 'i' is dotted and every 't' is crossed. And that's how it happened with this one. I didn't even know until I saw the song on the album that he wasn't taking a credit. But I sure know he did some writing on it. That's how it got done.

ON A GOOD DAY, YOU'RE SONGWRITING THE WHOLE TIME. —g

PLEASE OPERATOR
(COULD YOU TRACE THIS CALL)

By DEWAYNE BLACKWELL

G: My chance to write more with Dewayne Blackwell has come and gone. But one of the best times I've ever had was working with Dewayne Blackwell on a thing called "Anybody but Bill." We were laughing so hard. The next morning you get up, and though it's usually never as funny as the day before, that one was just as good the following day. It was a blast. Even the stuff we didn't put in there was just so good. We were writing on "Anybody but Bill" when he played me "Please Operator." I think we were dying we were laughing so hard.

ALLEN REYNOLDS: "Please Operator," this is another one of those tongue-in-cheek drinking songs that Dewayne Blackwell wrote with such mastery. Dewayne's just a great songwriter, and one who's had hit songs over many years. This one's kind of typical of Dewayne's sense of humor. Of course, he's co-writer on "Friends in Low Places," "Mr. Blue," "Nobody Gets Off in This Town." Garth and Dewayne were already friends when Garth and I first met.

THESE GUYS WOULD **NOT** SETTLE. —g

Dewayne Blackwell and Larry Bastian

G: Dewayne Blackwell is a pure rhymer. "Time" and "line" wouldn't work. It had to be "time" and "dime," or "time" and "rhyme." It had to be that way. Dewayne and Larry Bastian, these guys would not settle. They also knew that every syllable was percussive. Fell on the beat or pushed the beat. That's what these guys did. They did "Nobody Gets Off in This Town." If you look at that, it's all pure rhymes, all the way through, and all very rhythmic.

I GREW UP DURING THE **TYRANNY OF RHYME.**

—Larry Bastian

LARRY BASTIAN: If Dewayne wrote it, I can guarantee you one thing, it will rhyme. Dewayne never wrote anything, nothing I've ever heard, that wasn't filled with perfect rhymes. We're from the '50s and '60s, and there was a lot of Sinatra and Tony Bennett, Bing Crosby, Dean Martin, Marty Robbins. I always say I grew up during the tyranny of rhyme. Everything had to be a perfect rhyme back then. I wrote several songs with Dewayne. "Nobody Gets Off in This Town" was one of them. We had a good run. I think we wrote like twenty-two songs.

G: The guy is truly a gifted songwriter because he's aces in all departments. He knows what's commercial, what will rise out of a verse, what will meter right, what will rhyme perfectly, and what will communicate in the most direct way possible. He does it all. And leaves you laughing, while still getting at some core human truth.

TRISHA YEARWOOD: "Please Operator"? Garth has the ability to get such a mix of different songs on the same album, without losing a sense for the whole. He can get this on the same album with a song like "Last Night I Had the Strangest Dream," which feels like a poem set to music, a really deep song. And "Please Operator," with those harmonies, is such a classic country song, with such a clever lyric. I love that song.

Dewayne Blackwell and Garth

G: When he played me "Please Operator," I thought it was just brilliant. "I had to ask myself where would I be / if I was out drinking and if I were me / Then I thumb nailed the label and there I appeared / hiding out in a bottle behind a three-day-old beard." Wow. What a way to tell that story. Mike Chapman was the one who said, "Bubba," he goes. "This is a hit for you." But for whatever reason, it went into the vault. When you went back digging for *The Lost Sessions*, though, it was fun to have this one waiting for you.

MY BABY NO ESTÁ AQUÍ

By DAVID STEPHENSON & SHANE BROOKS

G: David Stephenson was one of those guys that was among the first to help me out when I was in town. Really good writer. Another guy from the Lone Star State.

DAVID STEPHENSON: I moved to town '85 or '86, from Texas. I'd had a few cuts; Janie Fricke was one. So, I'd met Bob Doyle at ASCAP. He'd signed Garth and two or three others. Garth was singing at a few writers' nights, so I'd heard him, but I first met him over at Bob's office. He'd been here probably a year or so, singing on demos and stuff.

G: I got to do a lot of demos for David back when I was a demo singer.

DAVID STEPHENSON: I was using another demo singer, having some issues. Garth said, "Man, I can sing them." So, he came over, but the songs were actually in too high of a key. It took Garth a while because he was trying to hit the notes. He could've played guitar and done the whole thing over in 10 minutes, but we just worked on it. After the demo session, he called me back and said, "Man, it took me too long, so I want to send you the check you gave me, and I'm not sure of the address." I said, "No, you cash that check. You spent the time on it." He said, "Well, as long as I live in this town, you have a free demo singer." So, I had him sing two or three other things the next year or so, and he wouldn't let me pay him. Among the artists that I've worked with, he's got the most untarnished reputation because of practices like that.

G: David was always positive…but honest. There'd be a big song on the radio, and he'd go, "That's the biggest pile of shit you ever heard, isn't it?" Real honest. I liked that. But then you'd talk about a George Strait song, and he'd go, "There's no better than that." He knew his country music inside and out. We kind of saw eye to eye.

DAVID STEPHENSON: Garth and I wrote a thing for *No Fences*. It actually was one of the two songs that didn't make that album: "It's

ISN'T THAT THE BIGGEST PILE OF SHIT YOU'VE EVER HEARD?

—David Stephenson

Garth with David Stephenson

Getting Hard to Keep Your Memory Alive." It's never come out. When I heard about *The Lost Sessions*, I was just thinking he might put that

I THINK OF BENNY HILL AND BUCK OWENS, BACKED BY THE TEXAS TORNADOS.

—**David Stephenson**

song on. But "My Baby No Está Aquí" ended up making it. I think of "My Baby No Está Aquí" as Benny Hill and Buck Owens, backed by the Texas Tornados.

G: I loved finding things like "My Baby No Está Aquí." This one's a dance song for me. Like "Cherokee Maiden" for Haggard. Or "80 Proof Bottle of Tear Stopper" by George Strait. Just a great two-step song. It's so cleverly written. "My baby no esta aqui no more / I used to be her number one vaquero / her numero uno caballero / But I had to hock my spurs and my sombrero / because when she left she took all my dinero." It's fabulous. He mixes English and Spanish, and it just works so well. It's just his upbringing. I think he was one of the best song-writers I've ever met in this town. I scratch my head, wondering why he doesn't have 1,800 No. 1s.

DAVID STEPHENSON: My wife worked at Columbia Records for years. They'd have a Christmas party for the women that worked in the office, and the men didn't come most of the time. I took Susan over, went to a movie or something, but when I was going to pick her up, I started writing that song. I said, "My baby no está aquí." Being from Texas, as I was writing it, I was just sticking English and Spanish all through the thing. Shane Brooks threw out the lines "She said I was her number one vaquero / numero uno caballero," the first two of the second verse. He became a writer on it for that.

CHRIS LEUZINGER: It's got that almost Cajun kind of vibe to it, which is great. A fun track, and the band really puts that across. Not too perfectly, though, because Garth and Allen liked it to feel real, live. Milton and Mike, when they break into a feel like this, they just groove together. They started playing together in bands as teenagers, knew each other since elementary school. They're like one thing. With two heads.

MILTON SLEDGE: I played on the demo of this song for David Stephenson, for his publishing company. So, I was familiar with it. I just loved the Latin feel. I'm a sucker for a good Latin feel. A lot of that is filtered up through New Orleans. All those early New York Records, like the R&B stuff on Atlantic, had a lot of jazz drummers who played swing in New York City Latin bands. When they did recording sessions, that feel was one of their tools. I was in the Army Band for three years, playing

THEY'RE LIKE ONE THING.
WITH TWO HEADS.

—Chris Leuzinger

Garth and Chris Leuzinger

a lot of jazz band stuff, so all that swing stuff and the Latin stuff is borrowed from those experiences, too. "My Baby No Está Aquí" let me pull some of that out.

DAVID STEPHENSON: Probably two or three years after Garth recorded it for Ty England's record, Bruce Bouton, the steel player on all of Garth's records, said, "I think we retracked that Cajun kind of song the other day, but don't get your hopes up, of course, because we probably overcut." Maybe that was *Scarecrow*? Years go by, and someone called me one day, and they were checking on the publishing information for "My Baby No Está Aquí." I figured some independent label or something heard it off of Ty's record and was wanting to cut it. I said, "Well, who's the artist?" And they said, "Garth Brooks." I said, "Well, that's good news!" Then he called me not long after that and had me come by the studio. He played it for me and showed me the song title on the mock-up of the CD cover. He said, "Here's your song."

G: I wanted to cut it so bad myself. We went back into the vault and got Ty's track, but it wasn't the right key for me. So, we recut the thing but kept the performance close to what we'd done first time around. Just felt so good.

DAVID STEPHENSON: I was there at Garth's first album release party. It was in a little rehearsal hall, a small room with maybe fifty people. I'd heard him at writers' nights and all those things, but I'd never heard him with a band. It was the guys that played on the record. They played the album but ended with "Keep Your Hands to Yourself." I remember just looking at Susan and saying, "Wow. All bets are off now." The energy was amazing. You just felt like something big was coming. When he put out "My Baby No Está Aquí," I told him, "You saved my life." And of course he said, "No, I didn't." I said, "Yeah, you did. Thank you." It was great. Whenever you get a cut, you feel like you're validated a little bit. You think, "Man, I need to write a few more songs." When it's a Garth cut, it feels even better than that.

Garth and Milton Sledge

LAST NIGHT I HAD THE STRANGEST DREAM

By ED McCURDY

G: I first heard this one on an Arlo Guthrie album called *One Night*. The album was nine cuts, seven on the first side, then you flipped it over and heard "The Story of Reuben Clamzo & His Strange Daughter in the Key of A." That

Mark Miller and Allen Reynolds

track was over seventeen minutes long. It was fabulous. Then the album ends with "Last Night I Had the Strangest Dream." I wore that record out. It's all live. It just grabbed me. That voice just pulls you in.

TRISHA YEARWOOD: The last cut on every album, for me and for him, it's that song that you just don't want to hear anything after. That's the song you end with. You want to leave people thinking, or it's a statement you want to make. Or it's just so emotional or stark that you don't want to hear anything come on after it. "Last Night I Had the Strangest Dream" is really about us loving one another. And that's kind of the song you don't want anything to come after. There are a handful of those songs, and you're lucky when you find them.

G: One thing I love about "Last Night I Had the Strangest Dream" is that of all the songs on *The Lost Sessions*, it's the one I've known the longest. Arlo's One Night must have been one of my dad's records. "Good Ride Cowboy" was the newest on *The Lost Sessions*, and it started things out, then the oldest song that I knew on the collection ended it. So, *The Lost Sessions* kind of spans everything in between those two.

ALLEN REYNOLDS: I've always adored that song, and I know Garth did too. In fact, I think on his first trip to England he sang it on a TV appearance. It was just Garth there with his backup singers. It's a perennial favorite.

MARK MILLER: I remember hearing that song "Last Night I Had the Strangest Dream" done by Simon and Garfunkel, in 1963, I think. I just love it, such a great story. Part of what I love about Garth's version is that Allen sings bass on it, along with Trisha and Garth. Just the three of them. It's a beautiful song.

G: We added Big Pal, Allen Reynolds. This might be the only record other than "How You Ever Gonna Know" that features Big Pal singing with us. That's him doing all the bass stuff. It's beautiful. Trisha cries every time she hears it because of the way Allen's voice comes through. It's just so pure. It was a joy making this record, the three of us bringing our voices together.

CHRIS LEUZINGER: It's another example of Garth and Allen just looking for great songs and being willing to look in unexpected places. Bobby Wood and Mark Casstevens really shine on this. And Mark put guitar *and* bouzouki on this. Bouzouki isn't something you hear every day, that's for sure.

G: It's kind of like a long-neck autoharp. And it sounds like that. Mark is doing guitar and then that bouzouki. Bobby Wood is on there, and then it's just me, Trisha, and Allen. I think the song was written in the '60s. It's kind of

THAT BALANCE IS HARDER TO GET THAN YOU CAN IMAGINE.

—Trisha Yearwood

a folk standard, really, and I enjoy that. It's deep, carries a lot of history within it.

TRISHA YEARWOOD: I don't think Garth would sit here and say, "Well, I don't care about being successful. I just want to cut the songs that move me." I mean, I think the best artists want both of those things to happen. You want to cut songs like this one, songs that move you, and still have commercial success. Garth's been able to do that beautifully. He has a really good knack at knowing what people want. He knows how to write songs that appeal to everybody. And he knows how to balance that with songs that are deeply personal and not always what people would expect. It all coexists, seamlessly, on these records. He achieves a balance that's harder to get to than you can imagine. But to get the full picture of the art, you have to listen to the whole story. It's the album that tells that whole story. And sometimes those deep cuts are the ones that will change your life, that you never would've heard if you didn't listen to the end. And there it is, waiting for you, the song you needed.

UNVEILING THE RING

G: So, Buck Owens decided to don his nightclub in Bakersfield, California, with statues of men of country music. Haggard, Jones, Strait, Bob Wills, Elvis, Willie, Cash, Hank Sr., and Buck himself. And for some reason, Buck included Garth Brooks in this list. Yeah, I don't know why either. (laughs)

FRED REISER: I met Garth when I owned the Crazy Horse in Santa Ana, California. Capacity 250. Garth was booked in 1989, had to cancel, but honored the booking, came back in 1990. By that time, Garth was, well, Garth. Ten thousand people showed up in our parking lot. I did a lottery, had a bullhorn calling out numbers. After selling the nightclub in the late '90s, I consulted for Buck Owens at his nightclub, the Crystal Palace, in Bakersfield, California. Around that time, Buck had decided he wanted to honor some of the male greats in country music.

G: There was a sculptor named Bill Rains who came to Oklahoma. He brought the guy that measures for a bronze cast.

FRED REISER: Bill Rains, from Billings, Montana, was the sculptor, a very country boy. He'd done a few statues in the lobby of the Crystal Palace, Bob Wills and Buck, and the people went crazy over them. So, Buck says, "I'm going to do more." That's when Garth and George Strait and George Jones and Haggard and the legends of country music became the idea. And that's when Garth got involved.

G: We pick the pose, take photos of everything, and Bill Rains goes back to Montana to do his thing.

FRED REISER: Buck was a very creative man, one. Two, a very good business-man. But he was quick to change his mind. So, if you worked with Buck, what he said this week might change next week. Going into the statue night, those eight to ten months out, I think the plan changed ten times.

G: Now, for some reason, I'm somewhere near Bill Rains's Montana studio and get to go see this statue before they fill the mold for it. What they do is make the statue, and then they put a mold around it and take the mold apart. Then they pour the bronze. When I see it, it's great, I love it. But Bill said, "I want you to be happy with this because once we do it, there's no turning back. This statue will stand for hundreds of years." And when he said this, it's like a hammer hit me in the head with that phrase "stand for hundreds of years." I said, "Can you put a wedding ring on it?" And he looked at me funny. I said, "Because I have a love that's going to do the same thing."

BOB DOYLE: This was a very big deal for Buck, but it became an even bigger deal for Garth.

FRED REISER: So, I was working with Garth, but I was working for Buck, and talk about a teeter-totter.

G: Well, before the unveiling, a few things have to happen. I had a chance, when Miss Yearwood was doing something in Cincinnati, an anthem or something, to fly down to Georgia to pick up her parents for an event we were all doing together. I have Jack and Gwen all to myself on a plane, and I ask them for their daughter's hand in marriage. This was in the spring of 2005, and I get their permission. And now I have to ask the three daughters.

TRISHA YEARWOOD: I would *love* to say I thought something was up…but honestly? I had no clue. (laughs)

G: Once I'm back in Oklahoma and we have the chance, I tell the girls to get dressed up for dinner. "What are we going to dinner for, Dad?" I said, "We'll go out tonight and I'll tell you." So, they're ten, eight, and six years old at this point. We're eating dinner, and we started talking about the future. And August or somebody said, "Dad, are you getting around to ask us about you marrying Trisha?" And I said, "Yes, I am." And they were all fine. I said, "But this conversation goes deeper than that. She doesn't have children, so if something happens to me, you have to take care of her. So, you three and Trisha are going to have to get married, as well. You'll exchange rings, vows, everything."

Now, I'm crying like a baby, but trying not to. I'm explaining how important it is that if something happens to me, that they take care of Miss Yearwood. Then Allie, at six years old, puts down her fork, looks at me, pats me on the arm, and says, "We got your back, bra strap." That was it. "We got your back, bra strap." Conversation over. (laughs) But that left me with the hardest one: I had to go ask Sandy.

BRYAN KENNEDY: That's just the way he thinks.

G: That was tough. But you have to ask, because if Sandy was getting remarried when the kids were little, I would've wanted her to do the same thing to me, come ask my opinion of the man that's going to be around our daughters. If Sandy would've said no, then that would've affected a lot of things. The brakes would've come on because we'd have to live together as a family. I chose to get married to Sandy; Sandy chose to get married to me. We chose to have children. What happens on the back side of those decisions we have to take responsibility for. I needed her blessing.

But I also needed to give her a moment to express whatever's needing to be said. And I thought she was going to do what I would do in her shoes, say something like, "Okay, but let me get some things off my chest first." But that's not what she did. She just said, "I think this is a good move for you, and I think it's a good move for our family." She was the better person in the conversation, and she was right.

BOB DOYLE: I think all of us would hope we would handle that moment the way they did.

G: So, now I'm going to get to ask the love of my life if she would marry me. So where am I going to do it? When we unveil the statue, she's going to see the wedding ring. It'll be the first thing she sees. I have my moment…then the phone rings.

FRED REISER: Close to the event, I called George Jones, and he said, "Ah, I don't know. I don't know how I'm going to get there." And Haggard was known for maybe not showing up the day of the event, and he was getting a little unsure. I was like the expectant father pacing the floor. Buck had said, "I want to make this an event of all events." Jim Shaw from the Buckaroos started by hiring the biggest stage, the largest jumbotron known at that time, and got a producer out of L.A. to do a six-camera shoot. So, this thing grew. Every week it grew, probably for the last six months prior to the event. But when it looked like we couldn't get George Jones, maybe not Haggard, Buck says, "Well, I'm going to have to reschedule it."

G: Fred's on the phone telling me that a couple of the guys can't make the date. I panic! The date has already been announced to the public, Trisha's parents already know, my dad knows, the Geisslers and LeFlores already know! So, I have to tell Fred what the plan is.

FRED REISER: Garth says, "Fred, you got to keep this a secret." I couldn't even tell Buck. We have to figure out how to handle Merle Haggard and George Jones. So, Garth hires a jet for George and his wife, Nancy, and another couple who came with them. And I make a deal with Haggard that he'll close the show—and he'll come there with his band by bus. But when Garth told me he was planning to propose to Trisha at Buck's place during the unveiling, I knew what I needed to do.

G: I think the answer ended up being flying George Jones out privately so he could get to the event. Whatever the answer was, we were on! Thanks to Fred Reiser.

FRED REISER: Buck didn't know, and I didn't tell anybody. I only told my wife what was going on, and she said, "Oh, my gosh, you're kidding." No one else found out, all the way up to the event, which just kept growing. Aside from Elvis and Bob Wills, who would be represented by Ray Benson, only George Strait couldn't get out of an existing commitment, couldn't cancel. Of course, if he had known what was happening, he might have done it anyway—but it was a secret I had to keep.

STORME WARREN: I was working for Headline Country then. When we got out to Bakersfield, there was a lot of press already there. And before the unveiling, the Crystal Palace held a press conference.

FRED REISER: Having these artists with Buck during the unveiling was definitely what I would call "press worthy," but the proposal during the unveiling was going to put the Crystal Palace on every homepage and every front page. I was honored to be a part of what was coming. I would do it all over again if I could. It was a personal thing for me. It wasn't a business thing, it was a personal thing.

G: We get out there, and Storme Warren—every time I see him, I still

Garth and Fred Reiser

laugh and go, "Fuck you Storme"—because in the press conference, he goes, "Hey, there's a wedding ring on the statue out there." And my answer to him was something like, "Well, I'm sure they made that statue from a photo, and we're not performing anymore, so it's probably from back in the '90s at some point." But he knows me too well. He figured it out.

STORME WARREN: (Laughing) I had to ask.

G: When they unveiled the statue, I took Miss Yearwood's hand. They've already unveiled Haggard, Jones, Strait…I mean this is pretty fricking cool. And I look at Trisha and point to that ring, and it was like everyone was there, but nobody was there but us. And then when you drop to one knee, it got so loud, but we were still just sitting there talking, the two of us. And the first thing she did was grab her face and start shaking her head from side to side, and I thought, "Oh shit, did I misread this one?"

TRISHA YEARWOOD: I know it must have scared him to death, but my first reaction was, "*No! This can't be happening in front of all these people! But yes! Yes! Yes!*

G: It was good. It was really good. It worked out really well. Her mom and dad were there. My dad was there. So, it was a good thing. The marriage was going to take place in Oklahoma. My dad was going to be the best man at my wedding. And the woman I will love for hundreds and hundreds of years was going to be my wife.… She was also going to marry three little girls.

MAKING HISTORY
THE ULTIMATE HITS

CHAPTER SEVEN

I HAD SPENT THE LAST TWO AND A HALF years with the guys from Walmart. They gave me *The Limited Series*, *The Entertainer* (a collection of live performances on DVD), and now it was time I gave them what they wanted...*The Ultimate Hits*. Again, no new album, no touring, just the songs they wanted. As much as I liked that plan, I know, the whole industry knows, you can't sell old music without new music. But I had been out of the business for a while, and this business changes every day, and we're talking *years* had gone by. But I only needed three things: I needed the song of songs, radio's full commitment to support an artist they hadn't heard from in years, and someone to pull all of this off. Truthfully, I just needed *one* thing...I needed a miracle. And it came in the form of a song.

MORE THAN A MEMORY

By LEE BRICE, BILLY MONTANA & KYLE JACOBS

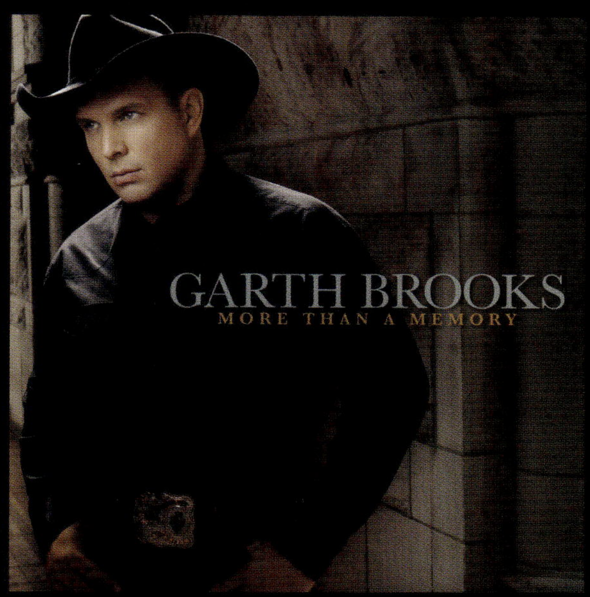

I **KNEW** GARTH WOULD NEED THE **BEST SONG.**

—Scot Sherrod

SCOTT BORCHETTA: Garth had called me in 2005 saying he wanted to do something but that he wasn't quite ready. So, in that moment I thought, "Wow, a chance to work with Garth….But he never called again." So, I was kind of bummed. He's got the best marketing mind, truly one of a kind. The idea of working on a project with him was really something exciting to me.

SCOT SHERROD: I was working for Garth's manager, Bob Doyle, at the time. I was a song plugger for Major Bob Music. We had these Monday morning meetings every week. Bob put the word out in the meeting that Garth was working on a new project, and that didn't happen very often. Usually, even before retirement, they'd have everything planned out and wouldn't say anything to us until everything was ready to go. Then Bob said Garth might even be looking for some new songs. I just remember thinking to myself after we left that meeting, "Man, I want to be a part of that."

SCOTT BORCHETTA: In the spring of 2007, Garth called me again, said, "Hey, I'm going to put out a new record, and I would love to meet with you." At that time, he was very much in retirement, but he had an idea of how to honor the promise he made to his daughters and fans but also fill what must have been his overwhelming desire to do music and maybe even play live.

SCOT SHERROD: As a song plugger, my job was to find opportunities for the company's songs. But when I got the idea that I'd really love to be the person to bring something in for this new project, I didn't really care where it came from. At the time, I was part of what's called a plugger's group. It's usually song pluggers from different companies that pull together, kind of a fun thing. I sent an email out to the group and told them Garth's looking for songs, so if anyone had anything good, well, let me hear it. So, I was looking everywhere, just wanted the best song. I knew Garth would need the best song. Drew Alexander was running Curb Publishing at the time. He hit me back and said, "Dude, you should send him the song from that CD I gave you." The CD had a few different Curb writers on there, including Lee Brice, Kyle Jacobs, and Billy Montana.

KYLE JACOBS: When I started hanging out with Lee Brice, there's this girl he just could not get out of his head. A first love thing. As songwriters, we're always looking for inspiration. What's it gonna be about? We probably wrote thirty songs about her. Eventually it got to a point where he was just tired of thinking of her so much, but his heart was still beating. He's like, "Kyle, I can't explain it, but she's more than a memory." I'm like, that's it, that's the one.

LEE BRICE: You should have seen me for a while there. I was writing a couple of hundred songs a year, and just about all of them were about her. When I look back, "More Than a Memory" is the one I was trying to write. It was the song I needed to write to be done with it all.

KYLE JACOBS: We got halfway through it and—Lee might kill me for saying this—I think he got a little emotional, like, we just had to pause. That was fine. But one day we had Billy Montana around and were like, "Hey, we got this verse and chorus, but what do you think?" Billy Montana was like, "Yup, I'm on it, let's go." He saved the day. He brought it home. All three of us did our parts, but he really helped just then.

BILLY MONTANA: We had had a weekly writers' meeting at Curb, and I remember Kyle and Lee coming up to me after the meeting and saying, "We got a song that we think you're the guy to help us write." I asked what they're calling it, and they said, "More Than a Memory."

> ## IT WAS THE SONG I NEEDED TO WRITE
> # TO BE DONE WITH IT ALL.
> —Lee Brice

I knew immediately what that meant. I love titles like that, where you don't have to do a lot of explanation, just have to keep the song on the rails. We went across the street to the writers' building, and I feel like it was the same day we finished it.

LEE BRICE: Then me and Kyle went over to Kyle's house to make a work tape, and that's when that big singing melody that happens in that chorus came. It wasn't until we got into the

LEE CRUSHED IT! IT WAS AMAZING!

—Kyle Jacobs

studio to do the work tape. I started ascending it out of nowhere. Then we got it on that little piano-guitar-vocal work tape, not even a proper demo.

KYLE JACOBS: Funny thing is, he had a big night the night before. He came in a little red-eyed, bloodshot, I'm like, "You okay? You got this?" He said, yeah, he was all right. So, I played piano, he played guitar, first thing in the morning. And I'll tell you, he sung his ass off. Just destroyed it. Crushed it! It was amazing!

SCOT SHERROD: I remember Drew playing that song at the song plugger's group meeting.

I knew the song, knew it was an awesome song, but at the time I thought Lee Brice had already cut it for his own project. I told Drew I'd totally send it to Garth, but I thought Lee recorded it already. Drew's like, "No, he hasn't." So, I sent it to Garth because it's so good, even just the work tape.

G: At this point, I'm not looking for songs, so I thought it was odd that Scot emails me this song, and I just click on it. It's "More Than a Memory." And I'm sitting there listening to the song, and my first thought is, "Shit, if I was still in the business, this is a smash." But as it turns out, Walmart said they were looking

Garth with Lee Brice

L to R: Drew Alexander, Colt Murski, Billy Montana, Garth Brooks, Lee Brice, Kyle Jacobs, and John Ozier at "More Than A Memory" #1 Party

for some new material for *The Ultimate Hits*. Walmart was one of the first retailers to use statistical research on steroids, so they had all these numbers showing what new music brought to greatest hits packages. So, the door opened. Walmart wanted new music, and I was staring at a new song I could sing the rest of my life.

LEE BRICE: I remember Rascal Flatts had put it on hold. I was on the road, about to walk into another radio station, when I heard that. This all happened really fast. I decided I was going to call and ask very respectfully if I could decline that hold, because it's just such a personal song to me, and I really wanted to sing it. Well, about that same time is when I got the call from Garth. He said a guy at his publisher, Scot Sherrod, who had no skin in the game at all, had heard this song through my guy at Curb. They were just trading songs, pluggers in town. But Garth called and was like, "I know that you got your thing going, that you're starting up, and this is a personal song, but I just wanted you to know I'd really love to record it if ever you decide not to." I mean, he's so respectful, it's ridiculous.

G: I had no interest in taking a song from a songwriter who might be set on recording it themselves. But I heard that demo, and I knew this was a special song.

LEE BRICE: Garth was my hero growing up. He was what I shot for when I was writing songs, when I was singing songs. I just loved that he went to the edge and beyond, spread that box out. When his stuff was coming out, it wasn't the normal country stuff. It had a power that just drew me to him. When I got the word that he was interested, and then he actually called me, it was pretty surreal, and to this day it's surreal. Things changed when Garth called, you know what I mean? I was like, yes, done.

SCOT SHERROD: I didn't think Garth would hit me back the same day I sent him the song. But he did, and I was like, "Okay, this is really cool." At that point I just told Drew. It went from there. Then Garth cut it, and he killed it.

G: My problem was, how are you going to better the demo? Lee Brice was the guy singing, and it was freaking awesome. It was a real simple demo, but the thing about a great voice is the less you put around it, the greater that voice gets. And he's singing the dogshit out of it! The only problem was, he didn't get back around to the chorus, which is a million-dollar piece of writing. The G-Men figured that one out in the recording studio. When that happened, in my eyes, the song was complete. Scott Borchetta came in and listened to that and the three other new pieces.

IN MY EYES, THE SONG WAS COMPLETE. —g

SCOTT BORCHETTA: Garth's studio, it's a block away. He gives me the tour. It's not a big, glamorous studio. It's like many studios on Music Row back in the day. It's a house. We've turned them into office buildings and studios. We go into the front lobby of the building, sit down, and he goes, "With this new package, I'm gonna do a few new songs. If we work together, you'll take care of them."

G: I turned to Scott to pick a single. I'd been out of the business for seven years. I don't have a clue what's going on. I can see what's happening in the industry. And I'm not liking what I'm seeing with iPods and downloads and illegal downloads and stuff like this. So, I'm already so far behind the industry, and it's already gone someplace I can't go. But this guy lives and breathes it. I just said, "You pick it." I felt "More Than a Memory" was going to be the one, so I was hoping that was the one he would pick.

SCOTT BORCHETTA: He says, "Hey, I'm going to do something I've never done before. You'll get to pick the single." First, I'm extremely excited, like, "Oh, my God." 'Cause there's four songs, and he's never let a record company into the studio before, let alone to pick the single.

HE'S NEVER LET A RECORD COMPANY IN THE STUDIO BEFORE, LET ALONE TO PICK THE SINGLE.

—Scott Borchetta

So, wow, okay. I go into the studio, he starts playing songs. I believe the second song he played was "More Than a Memory." I looked at him and said, "That's the single."

G: My whole career, the industry has told me I was crazy. I needed someone to say I was not.

SCOTT BORCHETTA: He said we should listen to them all one more time. "Garth," I say. "I promise it's 'More Than a Memory.'" (pause) I think he knew this.

G: It's one of those songs that kind of has it all: the story, the emotion, something we can all connect with. I wasn't coming out of

retirement, but this was going to be one hell of a good way to peek back through the door to where I came from. Then Scott had this idea to do something special for radio, for all those people who had supported me over so many years.

SCOTT BORCHETTA: There's a thing called CRS, Country Radio Seminar. I said to Garth, "It's been a few years since you've been in circulation, so there's some radio guys you don't know who don't know you. What if we put together GRS, Garth Radio Seminar? We can do it in one day." The idea was we'd bring in all your key program directors to Nashville for a one-day seminar. And pretty much every major company and program director agreed.

G: One day does it all? That was music to my ears. (laughs)

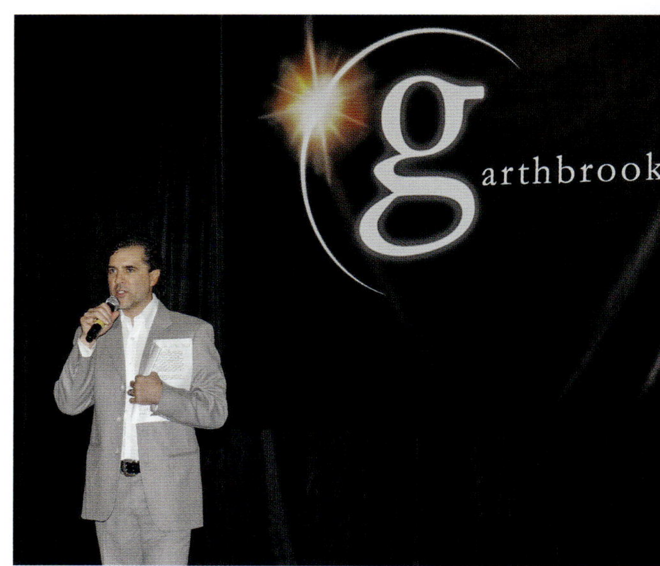

Scott Borchetta

SCOTT BORCHETTA: So, fast-forward to GRS. We've got everybody coming in. We're gonna do this at the Renaissance Hotel. We've got the biggest of the biggest and the best of the best. I call Garth, told him I want to run over how the show will go, the schedule. He goes, "Are you happy with it?" I told him yeah. He said, "I'm good." Click. He's doing his life

The G-Men

with his daughters. I would check in with him, briefly, once, twice a week, working one-on-one. I tell him we're going to do this GRS as if people don't know a thing about him, so when they leave Nashville they are going to know everything they need to know about Garth Brooks. Couple days away, I call and say, "Let me go over the schedule with you." He goes, "Pal, I gotta go." Click.

G: Soccer practices, school functions, the girls, they were always going to come firstEverybody knew this. They were patient with me. (laughs)

SCOTT BORCHETTA: So, we're a week out, same phone call. Garth says, "What time do I need to be there?" I tell him 8:30 a.m., that I'll meet him at the hotel's back loading dock. "Okay, gotta go!" Click. The night before, there's tons of excitement. In the morning, I'm waiting on the back loading dock. He's supposed to be there at 8:30 a.m., and we start rocking at 9 a.m. I'm just starting to sweat a little. I'm looking at the time, and it's after 8:30. He wouldn't let me schedule the specifics, but everybody's here, waiting. We have two huge album covers that we're going to reveal. We're gonna announce the live dates for charity he's planning to do in Kansas City as a part of this. But he's not here. Then, lo and behold, he

comes blasting through the gate in his dirty pickup truck, like he just got off the ranch, which he had. He jumps out, puts on his hat, says, "Hey pal, here we are! What are we doing?"

G: Scott did a beautiful job on all of this. He made it easy for me.

SCOTT BORCHETTA: I start going over the schedule, telling him this first hour is critical. "All right," he says. "What are we doing?" I tell him I'm going to do an intro speech, and then he's going to come out, talk, then we do the unveiling, he's going to announce the shows, and I'm going to play "More Than a Memory." He says, "Okay, you're going on first, right?" I say yes. "Well, stretch it out." So, I go on. Everybody's there. The stage looks fantastic. That room is full. I go into my thing. And I stretch it a little, just to do a few more minutes. Then, finally, here's the moment. If the magic comes into the room the way I think it's going to, this might be one of the best days of my career. "Ladies and gentlemen," I say, "please welcome…Garth Brooks." I turn, give him a handshake and hug mid-stage, and when I turn back around, it's a standing ovation. It was electric. It was the coolest thing, something I'll never forget. There was no one in that room who needed to be introduced to Garth Brooks. What a welcome back. Just electric.

G: That night we had a thing at the barn, all the radio folks. For one night, you had every radio programmer in America in there when Scott played them that song. It was a big riding barn that we had built for the girls. When we moved back to Oklahoma, we cemented the floor and parked all the stages from the world tours along with the buses and stuff. So, when these guys walked in, it looked like a party, and these radio guys got to come in and see all this.

SCOTT BORCHETTA: That night we went out to his barn. He had those three stages set up, and on each stage a video was playing of the concert done on that stage. The tour bus was there. All the gold and platinum albums were hung all the way around the barn. We walked in, and we didn't get thirty feet into the room, and it was over. Garth didn't move really for the rest of the night. No water or anything. Everybody's having the greatest time. He meets with every one of them.

G: The usual thing, of course, is that normally you'd tour behind a release. Radio stations can expect that when they add a single, they're going to see the artist come through, probably for a station visit, some ticket giveaways, all that. But here we were, introducing new music without any of the usual support from the artist. So, this was our night to say thank you, share some new music, without really knowing where it would all go. I still knew 90 percent of the radio people, even though I hadn't been in the business for years. These were the folks who made the '90s the decade it was for me. The men and women who did that were all there.

SCOTT BORCHETTA: Nobody left Nashville with music, only a memory. We played it for them but didn't give it to them to take back home. What we planned to do was, one week later, release the song to radio at midnight, so that every spin from the minute we released it would count toward the next week's *Billboard* chart. At the barn party, one of my radio friends told me he's going to add "More Than a Memory" right away in heavy rotation. That started this whole buzz throughout the room. People are coming up

to me like, "I'm gonna add it right out of the box. Right into power rotation." By the end of the night, the buzz was so massive. The rest of that weekend, going into Monday, it just kept going.

MANDY MCCORMACK: Garth had always done everything he could with and for radio. And you were starting to see the years of connection revealing itself. Like everyone missed this artist so much.

SCOTT BORCHETTA: John Zarling and I stayed at the office until 11 p.m. Sunday night Central, 12 Eastern, just to make sure that the record went off without a hitch, that it went through digitally, without one leak, and away it went. Then our phones started to ring. People are calling and freaking out. So, we stayed for probably another thirty minutes, high-fived. We wake up, we're the No. 1 song. It's the first time in history. Debuting at No. 1 in *Billboard*. We went through the week, and we were No. 1 by a mile. History. With an album you can project certain things. But with radio and coordinating so many stations, it's nearly impossible to forecast. I'll never forget that feeling. The first time in history, a No. 1 debut.

SCOT SHERROD: From my perspective— and you can ask any other song plugger or song publisher involved in what we do—there's so much talent out there. When it all comes together to the extent that it did with "More Than a Memory," I think everyone involved looks back and goes, dang, this is way bigger than us. A song found its way. Garth's a damn good songwriter himself, obviously, so for him to take the overall perspective that this is a team sport? If anybody could say it's about me, it's Garth Brooks. But he never has. "More Than a Memory" was a perfect storm and the perfect demonstration of how this can work when the music is the priority and teamwork is the emphasis. It was magical.

YOU STARTED TO SEE
THE YEARS OF
CONNECTION
REVEALING ITSELF.
—Mandy McCormack

WORKIN' FOR A LIVIN'

By HUEY LEWIS & CHRIS HAYES

G: I also got to record a couple extras for *The Ultimate Hits*, "Workin' for a Livin'" with Huey Lewis, "Midnight Sun," and "Leave a Light On." I loved all of them, and loved them enough to include them in there with the songs people already knew. I mean, just getting that chance to sing with Huey Lewis? C'mon.

HUEY LEWIS: I'd seen Garth perform in Germany, and it was pandemonium. He's such a great performer. So, I knew firsthand. I was on a fishing trip in Florida when I got the call about him covering "Workin' for a Livin'," and then he said he wanted to do it *with me.* That was a good day fishing.

THAT WAS A GOOD DAY FISHING.

—Huey Lewis

G: Huey Lewis got my attention when he's showing up everywhere and winning everything, but then he covers a Hank Williams Sr. tune. He covers "Honky Tonk Blues" and does it with real respect. You could just tell where he was coming from. Loved this guy anyway,

a blue-collar guy as honest as the day is long. But that sealed the deal for me.

HUEY LEWIS: Shortly after getting the call, I went to Nashville. We were recording at Garth's studio. There were all these country legends, just taking a real organic approach, no funny business, no samples. We even recorded our vocals live, and we did the same with my harmonica. It was a performance in the studio. Garth has a genuineness, a realness. His audience sings along with everything, probably because the performer's job is to call attention to everything that's there in that room—and nobody does that job better than Garth. He communicates. On the stage and in the studio.

G: What I loved about Huey when I met him was how he interacted with the other players. Artists are artists, but just like every quarterback wants to be an offensive lineman, every artist wants to be a musician. We all want to be the players. Huey's both. And it was really cool to see it happen between him and the G-Men. He started talking to the guys, and you saw the connection in their body language. He's the star in the room, but right then he's just one of the musicians. The musicians love him before we ever push record. And then when we pushed that record button, this guy came alive, and all the players came alive with him.

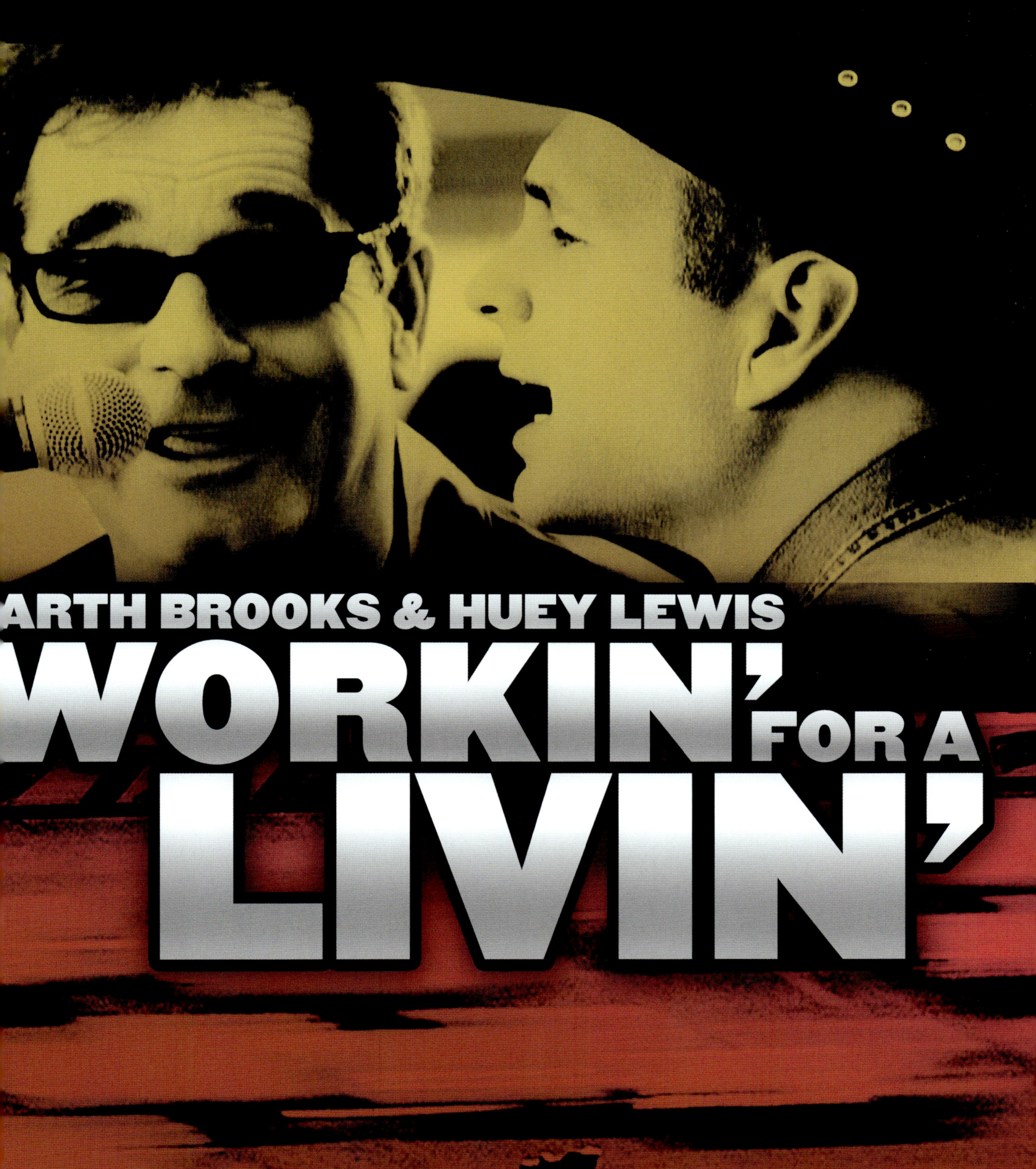
ARTH BROOKS & HUEY LEWIS
WORKIN' FOR A LIVIN'

The artist came in as a musician, and they loved him for that.

HUEY LEWIS: The recording session was great, and then making the video? That was another adventure altogether.

G: Now, my time with Huey alone was that video. This is where I really felt like I got to know the guy. He's like Blake Shelton, doesn't have a filter. He's just going to tell you what he thinks about the music business and everything else. You already worship him because he's just as down to earth as you hoped he'd be, an easy guy to fall in love with. Then you get to make a video with him at the Atlanta Speedway. It was crazy. I mean, I've done some stupid stuff—but I've never taken anyone with me.

But I'd always wanted to do that, had this idea for Trisha way back, NASCAR drivers going past at absurd speeds. Finally got to do it with Huey. Between the heat and the cars, I wasn't sure this was the best way to start a friendship. But I love what we came away with, and he was the best guy to do it with.

HUEY LEWIS: This was obviously a hard-working retired person. I always felt like a life is a great thing to have…especially if the career doesn't go so well. But there was Garth, having a life, and, obviously, most careers don't go as well as Garth's. He walked away from music to be with his daughters. That got my attention. He's one-of-a-kind. I could tell he was having fun dipping his toe back in, but I met him and knew it was just a toe.

MIDNIGHT SUN

By JERROD NIEMANN, RICHIE BROWN & GARTH BROOKS

G: "Workin' for a Livin'" had that up-tempo, pure fun thing, but "Midnight Sun" was the other fun one. It was something I wrote with Jerrod Niemann and Richie Brown. That got me my cowboy song and still kept the party going.

WHAT GEORGE DID FOR HIM,

GARTH DID FOR ME.

—Richie Brown

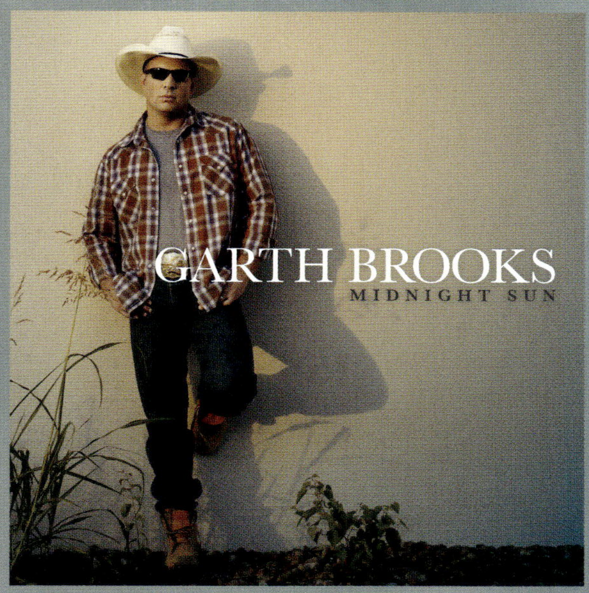

RICHIE BROWN: I was just a huge fan growing up. I mean "The Dance" is one of those songs, a part of your life. I'm from Texas, so I grew up listening to George Strait. When Garth came out, well, what George did for him is what he did for me. One of my buddies told me about him, and I started listening to him when I was in high school. This was just real country music.

JERROD NIEMANN: If they did a game show on Garth Brooks, Richie would be your phone-a-friend. I mean, he knows everything about Garth. Everything.

RICHIE BROWN: It was the songwriting that got me the most. Honestly, the Kim Williams songs and the Garth Brooks songs and things like that, these were what got me into wanting to write songs from the country side of things. I always used to tell people in Lubbock, Texas, that I was going to write with Garth Brooks someday.

G: Like I said, at the time, Bob Doyle was asking me to write with people outside our circle, to find some new writers to work with. Well, I think what Bob Doyle meant was writers that had No. 1s, but this guy Richie Brown had just moved to town two weeks before. He just seemed to be a real fresh guy who didn't have

I THINK OF GARTH AS A SONGWRITER FIRST.

—Bob Doyle

a lot of experience under his belt. Then one of the sweetest gifts I've ever been given was when Richie introduced me to Jerrod Niemann, one of the most talented guys I think I've ever met.

BOB DOYLE: This might sound strange, given what a remarkable entertainer and performer Garth is, but I think of him as a songwriter first. And Nashville songwriters, the ones who have long careers writing, sometimes just need new situations, new collaborations, to keep things fresh, moving, exciting. That applies to every writer. That's kind of what I was thinking.

JERROD NIEMANN: For "Midnight Sun," we went back to Oklahoma. But now he's got the big house built. It was the first time I saw a saltwater pool, a campfire in the living room. I mean, it was just what you'd want your hero to have. We wrote that song sitting around a campfire…*in his living room.*

RICHIE BROWN: It was a song about cowboy stuff. The whole "ain't no hay left on the ground / gonna join the sun sitting down." It was Garth who had this idea of working from that phrase "in the land of the midnight sun."

JERROD NIEMANN: I didn't understand what the phrase meant exactly. But where we grew up, it's just cowboy stuff—and I love it that way—so I connected with the images and where the song was heading. Then I got it.

G: It was fun to get with those guys. And try to remember, singing about honky-tonks? That's like me singing about breathing in and out, because there might be somebody who spent as much time in honky-tonks as I did, but nobody who spent more. "Midnight Sun" just had a natural place in there.

RICHIE BROWN: Sometimes the writing keeps going, right up to the end. Jerrod and I got a phone call from Garth, and he was like, "Look, I need y'all's help. I've got a couple of lines on 'Midnight Sun' that need a little work." I think he was in the studio recording. But he felt it wasn't perfect yet. We were at a bar down the street. We lived next door to each other at the time, built our houses with our "Good Ride Cowboy" money, basically. We closed out our tabs, came back here, and sat right where I'm sitting now, on my upper deck patio. We start trying to come up with lines for the second verse, where he thought it needed something. I think he used a little part of what we said. I'm not exactly sure, but it was really cool, because here he was cutting the song, still trying to make it better. No throw-away lines for him. That's a songwriter.

JERROD NIEMANN: For a minute there it seemed like "Midnight Sun" might be a single. What writer wouldn't want that? But "More Than a Memory"? What a song that was. I think Garth got it in one take, just a remarkable singer at work. But I'll tell you this: When he knew "Midnight Sun" was out of the running, he called us, told us directly. That's the kind of guy he is. Garth changed my life in so many ways. To be a part of *The Ultimate Hits* was an incredible experience.

LEAVE A LIGHT ON

By TOMMY SIMS & RANDY GOODRUM

G: "Leave a Light On" was going to be the last song on *The Ultimate Hits*. Tommy Sims wrote that with Randy Goodrum.

TOMMY SIMS: I remember the writing session itself like it was yesterday. The special thing about it for me was that I was getting to write with Randy Goodrum, who I'd been a fan of since childhood. So many of the songs that I grew up loving that he'd written, I didn't know he'd written them. But the ones I did know he wrote were Anne Murray's "You Needed Me," Steve Perry's "Foolish Heart," "Oh Sherrie." It was just song after song. Every time I'd encounter a Randy Goodrum song, it was so damn good. He became one of those names that stuck. When you're stacking up your heroes and trying to learn the craft, he was definitely in that bunch.

G: Tommy's got this unbelievable kind of soulful sound. And he goes places that you never predicted he would go in his vocals. That's "Leave a Light On."

TOMMY SIMS: I was very inspired by Elton John with that tune. The first part of it, what I brought to Randy, really felt like an Elton John type of song to me. I played him a couple, two or three bits of songs, just to see. But when I sat and played him that bit, he just right away went to the piano.

G: This was an amazing song to record and cut, because, like an Elton song, it just keeps layering and layering until finally there's a choir, strings, everything is going on. It was a really cool moment in the studio.

TOMMY SIMS: So, I was playing it on guitar for Randy. He goes to the piano, and, literally, as I finished the piece I had on guitar, he just

IT WAS AS IF THE SONG **HAD ALREADY BEEN WRITTEN.**

—Tommy Sims

started playing the next piece on the piano— it was as if the song had already been written, and we were just playing it together. It blew my mind. It was like, "Yeah, man. That's it. That's it." He kept saying to me, the rookie, "Man, are you sure? We can try a few more things." And I said, "No, what you just played! That's it." And that was it. It was that easy with him. You know that doesn't always happen.

G: I go to Allen Reynolds, say, "Hey, man, what would you think about this one, 'Leave a Light On,' if we're looking for a way to end these greatest hits?" Because we always end with something like "The Dance," a song that brings that kind of emotion. Allen agreed. It was the right way to end.

TOMMY SIMS: In Nashville, you would have to live on the moon to not know of Garth. The album with "We Shall Be Free" on it, my wife at the time and I just wore that sucker out in the

car, man. Everything I'd heard about him from mutual folks around town was that he was a good guy, which you love hearing about somebody who's riding so high. I was friends with the Kennedy family, with Gordon and Bryan. They were absolutely pivotal in my journey. I found Garth to be very, very similar to the Kennedys. Right off the bat I felt like Garth was a brother. It made sense to me that Garth and the Kennedys are close. I thought, well these are quality people who are drawn to each other, and these are the kind of people I want to meet and be around in this crazy business. It all made sense.

G: Tommy wrote "Change the World" with Gordon Kennedy and Wayne Kirkpatrick. Hell of a talent, hell of a guy.

TOMMY SIMS: Nobody had recorded "Leave a Light On." I think it had only been pitched once or twice. I think it was in the original batch of tunes that Janie West, my old publisher, had sent to Garth.

G: Janie West was one of those who, from the start, was not only in my corner…she helped build the corner!

TOMMY SIMS: I got a call from one of Garth's people saying, "Hey, Garth's heard this tune and wants to record it." And so, of course, it was all thumbs-up. "Leave a Light On" was in the batch of songs that were being discussed. I don't think anybody chooses songs for Garth. I don't think that ever happens. He has to hear it and feel it. This meant he'd said, "Yeah, I can get behind this." It was a really exciting time.

G: There was a song we cut at the end of the '90s called "When You Come Back to Me Again" that talks about a lighthouse. So, the lighthouse is kind of a symbol in our world, in the Garth fan base. "Leave a Light On," for me, connected to that imagery. I'd known the song for a while, but it seemed to be just a perfect way to end *The Ultimate Hits*. It's a serious song, balances out "Midnight Sun" and "Workin' for Livin'," which are really fun. We were lucky to find a smash like "More Than a Memory," but "Leave a Light On" took us out on the right note.

TOMMY SIMS: I was elated when I heard his version, man. Elated. My family probably got tired of me playing it for them. I was blown away. You write a song like that, but only in your wildest dreams do you imagine it might find a home with an artist like Garth. To have a guy like that connect to a song and lyric like that? You could not get any closer to a bull's-eye.

HE HAS TO
HEAR IT
AND
FEEL IT.
—Tommy Sims

BACK ONSTAGE...
BUT ONLY IN STAGES

CHAPTER EIGHT

DAVID PORTER: The week Walmart released *The Limited Series* box, we called it "the biggest day in music retail." Each box has six CDs in it, and I think it moved 500,000 boxes the first day. This meant 3 million CDs sold day one. The DVD tin came next, and then *The Ultimate Hits*…It was all a huge success for us.

G: So, I wanted to do a Walmart thank-you concert. David Porter says we can have our choice of Bentonville or Kansas City. Bentonville was close to the house, so I was like, "Hey, I'm fine with Bentonville." It was going to be just me and a guitar, a show for Walmart employees. And then we get a call from a guy named Tim Leiweke.

We developed a relationship through that, but I've got to tell you this: In my life, I've had a chance to meet a half dozen people who really affected who I am as a human being because of who they are as human beings, and Garth is one of them. This is a remarkable man with a remarkable soul.

BRENDA TINNEN: I worked with Tim Leiweke, and I'd seen the *Ropin' the Wind* tour years before. I loved this performer and his music. When Garth came to Staples Center in Los Angeles for a Teammates for Kids event, I was just watching his interactions with everyone, and, this might sound weird, but the fact that he took the time to speak to everyone

MIDWESTERN CULTURE
DOESN'T ALWAYS TRANSLATE
TO LOS ANGELES.

—Brenda Tinnen

TIM LEIWEKE: I'd known Garth for some time already. He'd done a good job of getting hockey teams to commit to his charity, Teammates for Kids, and I was involved with the Los Angeles Kings and the Staples Center.

and look everyone in the eyes and hold the door open for people going in and out, it was like, "Wow, this guy really, really impresses me." That kind of Midwestern culture doesn't always translate to Los Angeles. Here he was,

the highest-selling solo artist in the world, and he still took the time to interact with everyone. And he was just being Garth, right?

BOB DOYLE: This has always been Garth's style, as long as I've known him.

BRENDA TINNEN: A few years after I met Garth during that Teammates for Kids event, Tim Leiweke gave me a chance to come back to my hometown, Kansas City. AEG and the city of Kansas City were partnering to build a new entertainment venue, which was the cornerstone of a $6 billion redevelopment of the downtown. Tim asked me to be a part of building the arena. When I was asked who my dream artist might be for opening that venue, I told my colleagues, "I'd love to get Garth Brooks." And they responded in unison: "He's retired.

Garth with Brenda Tinnen

He's not touring." That was a refrain I kept hearing over and over.

G: We're thinking Bentonville for this thank-you show, which was a location not just close to me but to the Walmart corporate offices. But Tim Leiweke calls, and that's when I hear about this new venue being built in Kansas City. I figured I'd go see it. It seemed really serendipitous that they wanted to open their venue the

I kept asking Randy Phillips at AEG, the president and CEO. He said, "Well, he's just not touring." And I said, "Randy, I'm not asking for a tour. I'm just asking for him to come and open Sprint Center in Kansas City, Missouri." I knew Garth had a connection to Kansas City. His mother played there when she was in clubs, and Garth had done the Royals spring training camp. Randy—probably just to get me off the phone—goes, "You know, you might call

exact week that Walmart wanted the thank-you concerts. So maybe, I thought, it didn't have to be Bentonville.

BRENDA TINNEN: I was hearing, "Garth is not on tour" for a good eighteen months.

Steve Moore in Nashville. He's on the board for the Country Music Association. He probably knows Bob Doyle, and Bob might know more about Garth's availability." I called Steve Moore, and he laughed right out loud. But still, he said, "Well, your timing is good. I'm going to a dinner tonight for the CMAs, so I'll ask Bob if I see him." The next day I get a call from Steve saying, "You're not going to believe this. I walked into the dinner, and the first person I ran into was Bob Doyle. I told him I had this crazy lady in Kansas City that wants Garth to open her building."

G: I don't think any of this would have happened if it wasn't for a woman named Brenda

THIS WOULDN'T HAVE HAPPENED IF IT WEREN'T **FOR BRENDA TINNEN.** —g

Tinnen. She was tenacious. And more often than not, that's what it takes.

BOB DOYLE: As much as Garth wasn't touring or even playing dates, this was right up his alley.

BRENDA TINNEN: It must have been three, four months later that we had a temp answering the phone who comes running down to my office saying, "Brenda, there's a man on the phone that says he's Garth Brooks!" And I thought to myself, "I just know it's really him. This is what he's like. It's him."

G: So, Brenda tells me they're going to be opening the Sprint Center in Kansas City. And they want us to open it. Now, the initial idea was to have a thank-you show for all the Walmart employees. But in Kansas City, there weren't enough Walmart employees to fill

a venue the size of what they were building there. You would have to open it up to the public. But I figured I'd visit, see the venue, get a sense for what they have going on.

BRENDA TINNEN: I got a call from Ben Farrell, a promoter, saying, "Well, Garth's really thinking about this hard, wants to come to Kansas City to see the arena. But, Brenda, you can't tell anybody he's coming or was there."

I have been in this industry a very long time, and I have never had a potential performer ask to see the building. Usually it's the promoter, the artist's manager, or someone else. So, Garth comes. We showed him the arena, which you could see from our temporary offices. And he goes, "Oh, this really looks good. Can't wait to go see it." I said, "Garth, Ben Farrell made me promise that no one would know that you were in town." I mean, we were coming into completion and had our highest number of trades working on the job. I wasn't sure how Garth could see the venue up close without being seen himself.

G: I love visiting these places, learning about their construction from the people who build them. I've spent a lot of time in them. You work in these venues, and you work *with* them. It's where you meet your audience. And each venue has its own character.

BRENDA TINNEN: So, Garth insists on coming into this venue that's nearing the end of its construction, and he's wearing a hard hat and…*an orange sweatshirt*. I could already see some of the folks doing a double take as we come in. Then we go to where we can see the arena bowl, and he says, "I gotta say, it feels so good to be looking out at this again." It was then that I started thinking, "Oh, my God, we might have a shot here."

TRISHA YEARWOOD: Artists who stop touring, stop releasing new recordings each year, they can't expect to pick up where they left off. That's just not how it works. Garth understood this, and I think he accepted it, which couldn't have been easy. But he'd lived a big part of his life in venues. It was still alive in him. Step into a venue, and you're going to feel a rush, you know?

BRENDA TINNEN: Then Garth came out into the arena and, I'll tell you, it was the weirdest thing. All of a sudden, the entire arena just goes dead silent. All of the workers—and there must have been a thousand—come streaming out of the stands and start forming a line. And Garth stood there and spoke to each and every one of them. He signed their hard hats. He signed ceiling tiles. He took

THERE WERE PEOPLE WAITING FOR HIS RETURN, WHETHER GARTH BELIEVED IT OR NOT.

—Storme Warren

STORME WARREN: There were a lot of people, patient people, waiting for his return, whether Garth believed it or not.

BRENDA TINNEN: But you know what? None of the folks there that day said anything. It's like Garth had asked them not to, and those construction workers didn't leak a thing. Then—the next day, I think—I got a call from Ben Farrell, and he said, "It looks like we're doing this show." I can't tell you how that felt. It's a moment I won't ever

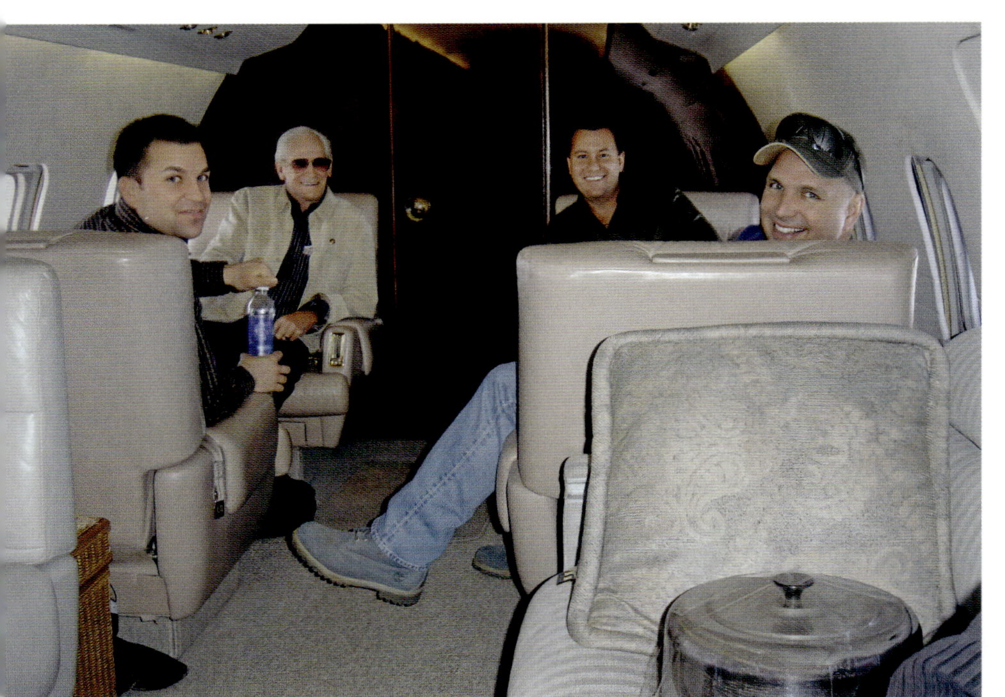

pictures with them, and they all were saying, "Oh, wow, are you going to *play* here?" I thought, "Ben is going to kill me. This is definitely not a secret."

forget. We were going to open the Kansas City Sprint Center with a Garth Brooks show. My dream. The date was going to be November 14. One show, one ticket price of $25.

TIM LEIWEKE: I said to Garth, "You don't understand the pent-up demand there is for you." He's like, "I don't think so, Tim. I'm not sure they remember me in the way you're thinking." I'm like, "Garth, you have no idea." He said, "Well, let's put the show up and see what happens."

BRENDA TINNEN: When the tickets went up, we were all on a conference call from Ticketmaster headquarters, Ben Farrell, obviously the Sprint Center and our box-office crew, and then Garth and Trisha. You could hear bacon crackling in the background. I'm not sure if it was Garth or Trisha cooking, but they were just getting ready to have breakfast. Garth thanked everybody for all the hard work to get us to that point. Then he said, "I really do hope we can sell out a show. I haven't been out there for so long, I'm not sure people remember me." That wasn't shtick. I mean, you could just tell how sincere he was.

G: When one artist leaves, another comes in. New faces, new songs. It's just a fact of the business.

BRENDA TINNEN: We had decided that Missouri and Kansas, the general Kansas City region, would get a few minutes' head start and that the internet sales would lag behind. I would say within sixty seconds, the first show, the November 14 show, was gone. Totally sold-out. Sixty seconds. And tickets still hadn't been opened to people buying on the internet.

TIM LEIWEKE: So it began. (laughs)

BRENDA TINNEN: Then Ben was speaking with Garth. They were trying to figure out if they thought they could sell out a second show. I was telling them how many people we still had in line. And there wasn't really a good way at that point in time to determine how many people were waiting to hit the internet. That just hadn't been developed at that point in time. Then Garth said he would do a second show. And then he told us Trisha had agreed to play the shows with him. Of course, we put that information out there as quickly as we could. Then we hit go again, and we waited—and I mean for a matter of seconds—and it sold out, again, in less than a minute.

IT WAS SOMETHING THAT
I HADN'T EVER
EXPERIENCED.
—Brenda Tinnen

TIM LEIWEKE: The first one led to the second one, led to the third one, led to the fourth one, led to the fifth one, led to the sixth one, led to the seventh one, led to the eighth one, and he could have kept on going, quite frankly.

The Geisslers and The LeFlores

BRENDA TINNEN: I am convinced, to this day, that we could have gone for another three, four, five shows. It was euphoric. Every time they announced another show out on the plaza, you could just hear this scream through all of downtown Kansas City. It was something that I hadn't ever experienced. And Garth hadn't even gone onstage yet! On the call, Garth finally said he was going to stop at nine, and he thanked everybody that was on the phone. But then he said, "Now, Brenda, when I'm in Kansas City, I want you to invite all of your folks. I'm going to do a special show for them, just for them." And it was like, are you kidding me? That was everybody who worked the on-sale and our families. A private show as a thank-you!

G: When we first started this, it was just going to be me and a guitar, doing a private thank-you show for Walmart. Well, this thing got out of hand really quick, and in such a great way. But we don't have the players ready, we don't have anything. It was all really rusty, but everybody was so sweet. And it gave me a chance to stand up there and be back with the audience who got me there in the first place.

WARREN ZANES: To be away from touring for ten years (Garth's last tour ended in November of '98.) is a remarkable thing for an artist who made his name on the stage. I can only imagine how stirring it must have been to feel the lights, the sound, the beautiful roar of the audience. What an emotional transition to negotiate, right? And then, just as suddenly, Garth and Trisha's new and dear friends in Oklahoma got to see this entirely different side of their friends' lives. I'm guessing that those friendships, particularly with the Geisslers and LeFlores, must have been like a kind of anchor in that moment, keeping Garth and Trisha tied to the life they'd created with the girls in Oklahoma. But for those new friends? What a trip.

WE WERE **TREATED LIKE FAMILY.**

—Lisa Geissler

LISA GEISSLER:
I remember going to the concerts and how we were treated like family. We were backstage and allowed to walk around, allowed to go anywhere. It was really cool to see the people that Garth surrounds himself with too, the band and crew. Because they're all amazing people. But Garth was just the same as he was at soccer practice.

KIM LEFLORE: At the time, I asked our son Wes— he was nine, maybe ten— if he wanted to see Garth in concert. He said, "I don't know that I want Taylor's dad to be my first concert." He had no idea, only knew that Garth was Taylor and Allie and August's dad.

JOE LEFLORE: Then, when he saw Garth onstage, Wes almost couldn't believe it was him. "That's really Garth," I said. "Same guy that drags us around behind the Jeep in the snow."

KIM LEFLORE: In my mind, I'm thinking, "Oh my gosh, the kids have no clue." I knew how big Garth was. But they found out when we went to Kansas City to see those shows. Garth and Trisha were like, "Come on, let's just jump on the plane. Let's go." We're like, "Holy cow."

TIM LEIWEKE: At the end of the day, he did this string of unbelievable nights of music where his fans all came together and had a celebration—a celebration about the fact that not only was Garth not gone, but he will never be gone, never be forgotten. The energy of those shows was just incredible. But I'll be honest with you, I didn't really get it until that moment. I thought I understood. But I didn't. Then I saw that. I think I went to all nine shows, and I remember looking at it going, "I cannot believe the relationship between this man and his fans, and how genuine it is.

IT WAS THRILLING FOR ALL OF US.

—Trisha Yearwood

Just no bullshit, pure, unadulterated joy, love, respect." You could tell how much he missed it, and how much they missed him.

BRENDA TINNEN: True to his word, Garth added a matinee on the Saturday show, just for the people who worked on the show and their families. I was like, "Garth, you have done so much for Kansas City. You don't have to do this. Everybody was thrilled to work on the show." But he set it up for Saturday afternoon. Garth and the whole band got up onstage, and he thanked everybody and said how great it was, how he appreciated their extra hard work. He

acknowledged several people. Then they played songs that meant something special to him, talking about every song that he was playing.

TRISHA YEARWOOD: It was the closest thing we experienced to Garth being back out. In the fourteen years, this was it. It was thrilling, for all of us.

BRENDA TINNEN: It wasn't the set list from the concerts that he did during the matinee. It was songs he'd heard in the car with his dad, or something his mom loved. He introduced all of his bandmates and Trisha and everyone. Then he got off the stage and went to the back of the arena floor where these merchandise tables were set up. He and his crew handed out shirts, hats, everything, to each and every person that was there, no charge. He gave people those indelible memories that you hold onto your entire life.

TIM LEIWEKE: I remember having a conversation with Phil Anschutz, who started and owned AEG. I told him, "Phil, music is the essence of our lives. We're born with it. We die with it. Through music we celebrate and mourn everything important in our lives, and if I've ever met anybody that is the epitome of how much music matters to us, it's Garth…and if you don't believe me, go to a Garth Brooks show and you'll see." In Kansas City I could see a flame reignited in him, some deep experience with his fans. You could tell. I felt like I knew there would be a moment he would come back. I thought, "He'll do it his way, his time, his place, but the greatest live artist of our time has to be out there performing live."

I COULD SEE
A FLAME
REIGNITED
IN HIM.
—Tim Leiweke
BROOKS
7

GETTING OUT THERE TO GIVE SOMETHING BACK

THE FIRE AND FLOOD RELIEF SHOWS

CHAPTER NINE

BRENDA TINNEN: To this day, I'll see people in Kansas City when I'm out and about, and they'll say, "Oh, you brought Garth to Kansas City. Thank you so much." Then they'll tell me a story about something magical that happened to them the night they saw him in 2007. What has that been, 15, 16 years? I still get those comments. Garth changed many lives in Kansas City, put Kansas City on the map. What was hard to believe was that he didn't come out of retirement after that. He went back to his farm to raise those girls with Trisha. But not before he did one more thing with us. Because as the shows in Kansas City were happening, there were wildfires raging out of control in California.

YOU JUST WANT TO HELP. —g

G: We were probably in show two of nine at the Sprint Center, working with the AEG team that was based in California, and we're spending all day before the show watching on the television as California burns in the

Southern California wildfires. Tim Leiweke is right on my shoulder and says, "Garth if we give you the Staples Center in Los Angeles, will you come play a benefit to help with the California wildfires?"

TIM LEIWEKE: No, Garth came to me. I didn't go to him. I know how this happened. But I immediately jumped on it. Southern California was in the middle of a really tough period of time. We were beginning to see the impact of what's going on around us with the climate, and we were having terrible fires, especially down in the San Diego area. Unlike some of the fire danger we have here, where we're always able to contain it, we were not able to contain this fire. And it was multiple fires.

G: Tim will probably tell you this wasn't his idea…but I'm in retirement. I'm totally happy at home. Yes, I miss touring, I miss music, but nothing can compare to being a dad, not even close. But you see what's happening in California while you are hanging with the people who can make a difference, and you just want to help.

TIM LEIWEKE: The fire grew and took out homes and people's lives. We lost firefighters, the men and women who protect us. We needed to get them new equipment and do something to honor the people we lost.

G: I told Tim I wanted to help, but I need help figuring out how to do that.

TIM LEIWEKE: He didn't want to confuse anyone if he was retired or not. Then he said the only way he could see it working was if the ask came from someone directly tied to the State of California.

G: Here comes a letter from Governor Schwarzenegger. I say yes, let's do this.

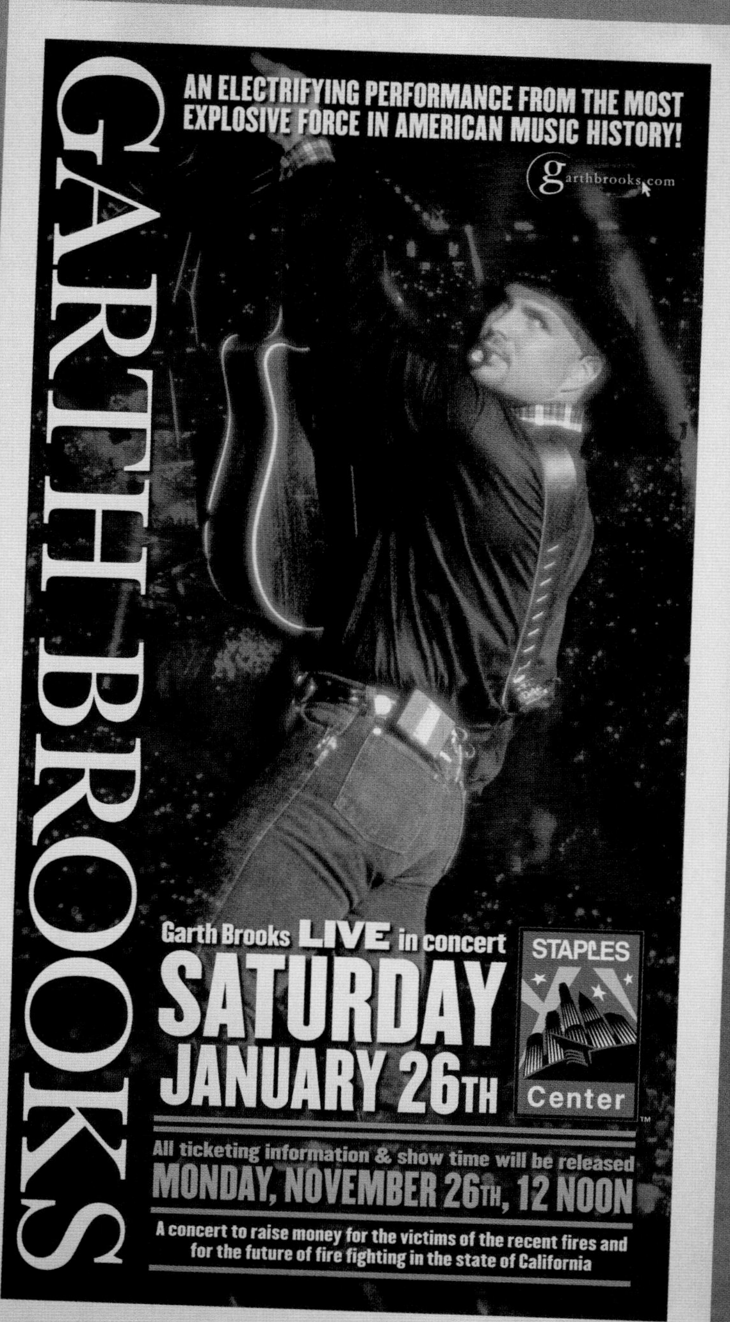

BRENDA TINNEN: Tim spoke to someone at the Staples Center, and they said, "Well, we only have two days where the building's not booked." I just nonchalantly said, "Well, the changeover crew there is great, because in two days on a weekend, Saturday, Sunday, there would be three basketball games and a hockey game." Then Tim said, "Well, yeah, and on Disney days we do three shows on a Saturday."

G: I suggested Saturday night would be the best bet. If we go two, we make the second show Friday night. After seeing what happened in K.C. *and* this was a fundraiser for what the state was going through at the time, we made a plan for possibly *five* shows total over two days.

BRENDA TINNEN: Which is insane.

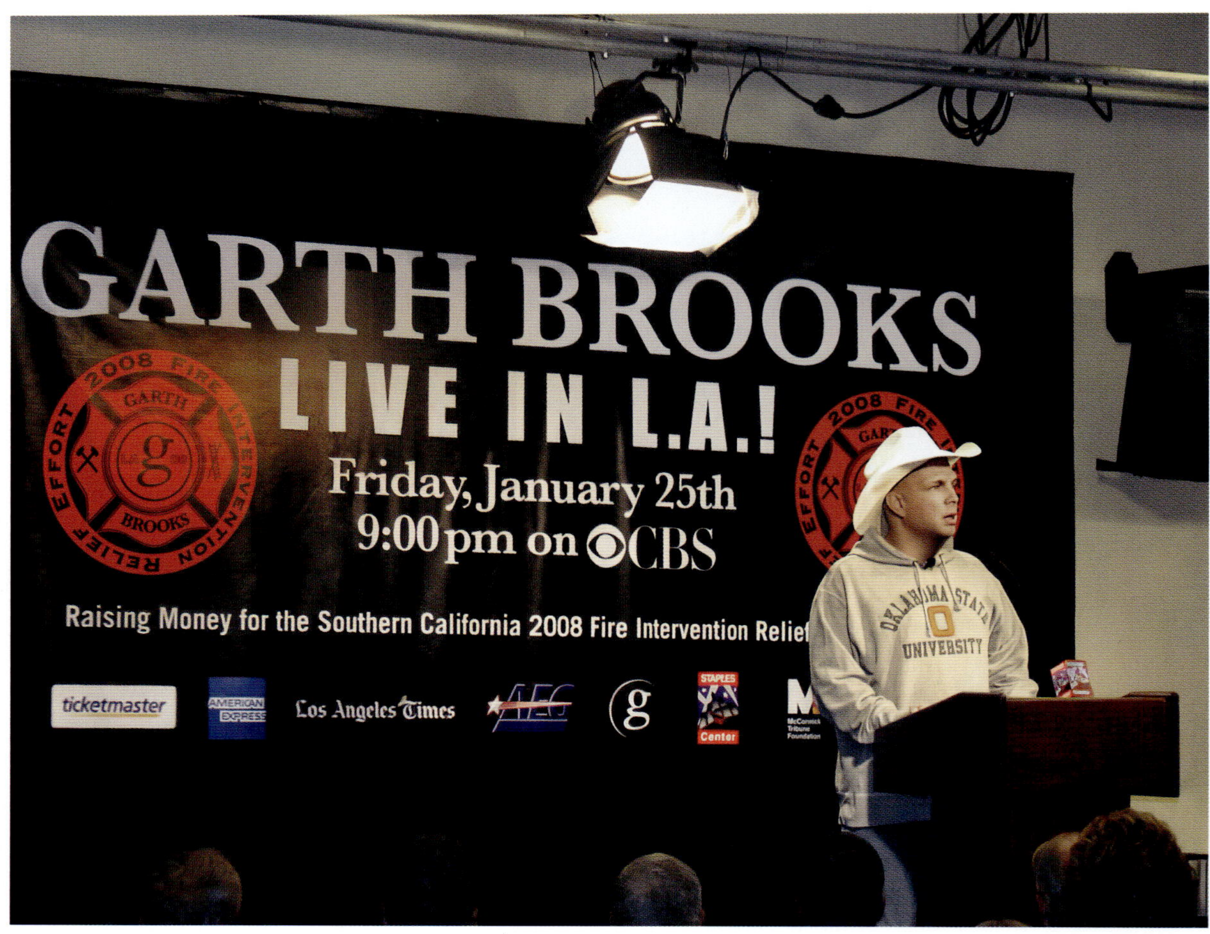

YOU CAN'T DO FIVE SHOWS IN TWO DAYS.

—Tim Leiweke

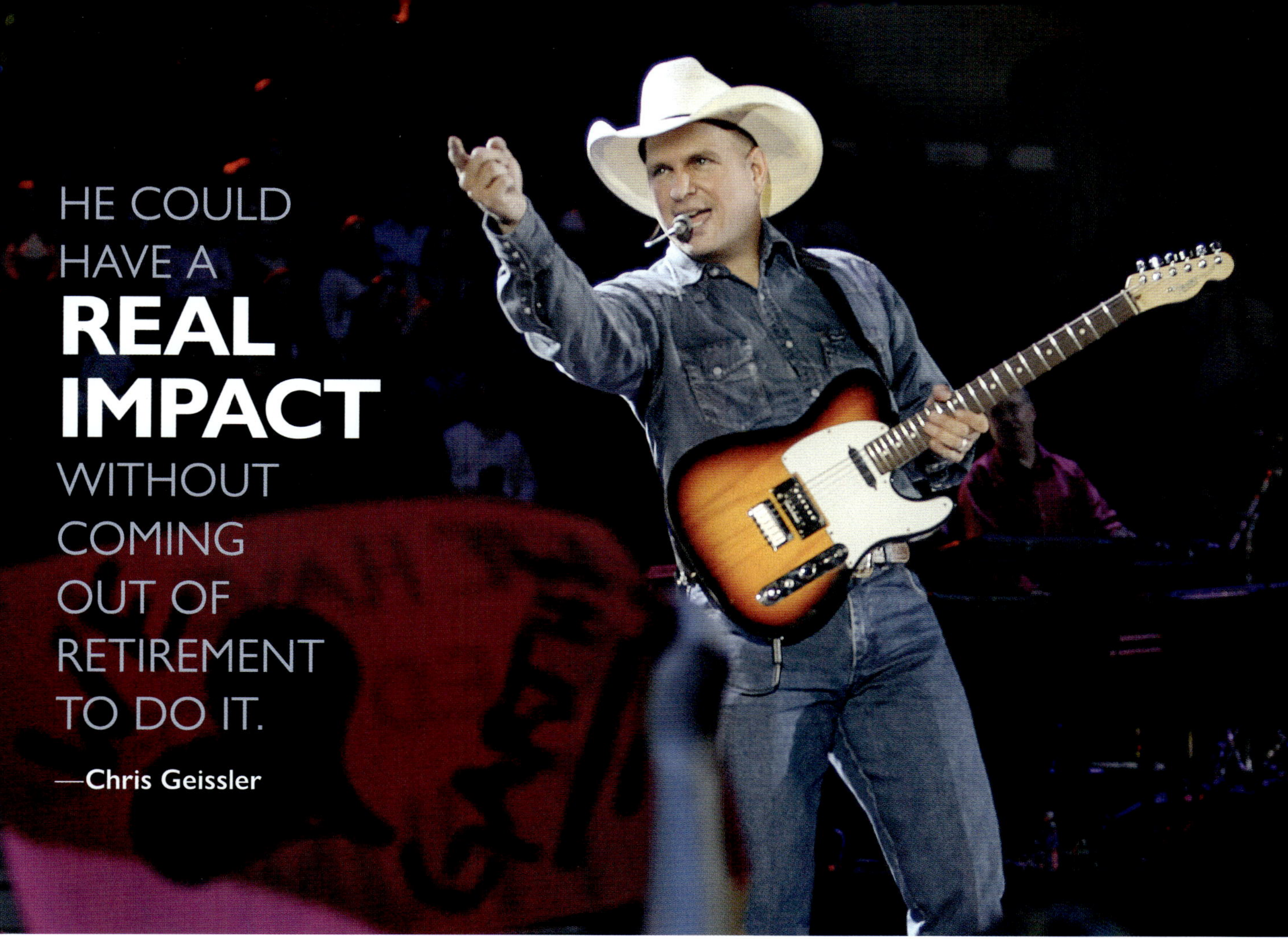

TIM LEIWEKE: I said, "Garth, you can't do five shows in two days." He's like, "I got it. I got it. We're good." I say, "Let me make sure I got this straight. You want to do five shows in about twenty-four hours?" He said, "Come on, partner, we need to help." And he did it, and the energy was full-on beginning to end. You can't go into ideas and partnerships with Garth and be half-hearted, man. You've got to be committed. Because when Garth does something, *he's* committed, and most of the time when he does something, it's to help somebody else.

CHRIS GEISSLER: We knew Garth was a hard worker, but, after years of friendship, watching him on the farm, we got to see what that hard work looked like when it wasn't on a farm and it was in an arena. It blew our minds. But I think he saw that people needed help, and he could have a real impact, without coming out of retirement to do it.

TIM LEIWEKE: We raised $8 million. We were fortunate enough to have the McCormack Foundation in our lives. They committed to matching every dollar we raised, and we were off. At the end of the show on Saturday night, I was so overwhelmed just by the magnitude of what this man had done, and by the time and the energy he had put into it. I went backstage to give him a hug…and he's doing laps up and down the hall at the end of that fifth show, because his adrenaline is running so high. I'm looking at him like, "Dude, most people would be lying in a heap somewhere on the side." But I think that soul of his had realized what he had done, especially on Friday night, when we had the firefighters and the families of those we'd lost there for the show. It was moving, just so emotional. I mean, *$16 million* to buy new equipment for firefighters in Southern California who were fighting against all odds.

THIS THING...

LOS ANGELES
COUNTY
FIRE
DEPARTMENT

...MAY NOT BE OVER. –g
2008 FIRE INTERVENTION RELIEF EFFORT
GARTH BROOKS
LA 08

G: I can't even define it. It's euphoric. These shows make me believe this flame is not dead. I have no plans on returning to touring again, but I see what David Porter saw three years

TENNESSEE
WAS ON ITS OWN. —g

earlier. This thing may not be over. Those shows were phenomenal, meant so much to me. That 10:30 show on Friday, with the firefighters and their families in the audience, will stay with me forever. That was the show for me.

TIM LEIWEKE: He's kind of like a power station, right? There's so much energy he

generates. This isn't a guy out trying to buy yachts. That's what I love about him the most. It's always about his fans. It's about the cause. It's about the need. It was remarkable.

G: We all go back home when it's over, and everything is great. We're raising our babies. But what we did for the wildfires came back to our minds when, just a few years later, Nashville gets hit with the flood of the ages. It made it hard to see that Interstate 65 was so far underwater that the cars that were stalled out on the highway were passed *by a church* on their right. There's so much water in this place that they called it a hundred-year flood…but it was like nothing we'd ever seen. But the nation's eyes are on a ruptured oil rig off the Gulf Coast, which meant Tennessee was on its own.

EVERYONE WAS THERE
FOR THE RIGHT REASONS. —g

WARREN ZANES: What I find the most striking is that Garth stayed true to his commitment to remain in retirement to raise his daughters but also stayed true to the man he is, which meant that he would go back out to play if, in his view, the situation called for it. He didn't do it because he loved to perform as much as he does—that was just the gravy. He did it because it could make a difference in a crisis…and this crisis was Nashville. The Nashville shows brought in some $5 million. It just so happened that he got to do what he loves as he set out to help a lot of people. But then he got back to what he'd committed to doing: being a present father.

G: The call goes out to the industry to help with these floods, and everybody comes. McGraw, Urban, everyone. There wasn't anybody who wasn't helping. And that meant all the crews, venues, subs, you name it. They're all putting on concerts; they're all pitching in. This is in May. The country music industry would raise a *lot* of money. But we knew they'd be through that money in no time because the need was so great. We decide that if we're going to help, we're going to do it at Christmas. The relief effort is going to need it then.

BOB DOYLE: And that was exactly what happened: The relief effort needed more money, badly.

G: We got with a woman named Ellen Lehman, who said let's make sure every penny is going to the flood survivors. It was her idea to create a board made up only of flood victims. So, the board members agreed not to take a penny of the money. We raised some money and got it to the people who needed it.

TRISHA YEARWOOD: It may be one of my very favorite experiences in Nashville. It made Christmas something deeper, something so closely tied to what the spirit of Christmas should be.

G: Nine sold-out shows. For a guy that was so out of shape and not expecting it, it was rough. But I learned that I didn't have to make it

IT MADE CHRISTMAS SOMETHING DEEPER.

—**Trisha Yearwood**

through nine shows on my own. I really learned it when I looked out there at the audience and said, "I'm going to need you to sing for me. I'm going to need you to help." Boom! Man, the sound of applause…and then the singing came. It was beautiful. Everyone sang. Everyone was there for the right reasons. And those nine shows changed everything for me. To this day, if people tell me they were at the Nashville Flood Relief shows, I say, don't come to any other show. It doesn't get more beautiful than that.

VIVA LAS VEGAS

THE GARTH BROOKS THEATER

CHAPTER TEN

BOB DOYLE: The Las Vegas thing wasn't planned. There was no long-range vision that this came out of. There was a lot of chance involved. Obviously, Garth was in retirement.

G: In 2001, the touring was over, appearances, making records…all that was over. But everything else related to being a celebrity did not stop. The foundation work, the charity work, that isn't over. And 90 percent of our foundation work was celebrated by summer and winter thank-you parties in Vegas for the athletes who donated to the foundation. This went on the entire decade.

STEVE WYNN: That's how Vegas happened.

BOB DOYLE: I took a call with Steve. He talked to me a little about who he was, what he was doing in Las Vegas. He was very aware of Garth. I'll never forget this: I'm telling Steve that Garth is very event-oriented. Steve says, "Bob, I know events. I did the Rat Pack with Frank Sinatra, Dean Martin, Sammy Davis Jr." I went, "Okay, you know events (laughs). Let me talk to Garth, and we'll get back to you."

G: I had wanted to get with Steve Wynn because I needed Wynn to help me with my foundation in Vegas. I write an email saying that to Bob Doyle, but before I can hit send, Bob sends me an email that just says "Steve Wynn" on the subject line. I'm thinking, *Well, this is crazy.* In the message it said, "Steve Wynn is looking for you. Here's his number." I'm feeling like someone is screwing with me, because this is…this is perfect. And then I look at his phone number and it's something like out of ten possible numbers, *seven* of them were *sevens*! Seven is my number, so I'm thinking this is my guy right here. I call him up, and he's great. He definitely knew his country music.

STEVE WYNN: When I was thirty years old, in 1972, I got control of the Golden Nugget on Fremont Street in Las Vegas and redid it. In 1973, at Christmas, when the remodeling was finished, with the new, revitalized Golden Nugget taking up the full block on Fremont Street, I had a thing called the Gold Strike Lounge. The Gold Strike Lounge sat about two hundred people and was open to the casino

SOMEONE IS SCREWING WITH ME. —g

with a stage at the back wall and a bar out front in the casino. The Golden Nugget had scale acts in that same space over the years, but I had redecorated it and reconfigured it as the Gold Strike Lounge. I knew that entertainment was always the key in Las Vegas, and I wanted to upgrade the entertainment.

BOB DOYLE: Steve understood the difference a great entertainer could make.

STEVE WYNN: I had an entertainment director named Jimmy Dean, not the singer. Jimmy came to me and said, "Steve, we could carve out a place for ourselves with country music. It's big now, especially underground country, Waylon Jennings, and people like that." So, Jimmy and I went down to the CMAs, got some hotel rooms, put on our cowboy boots and jeans, and tried to blend in. I was a Jewish country guy. But I was a roper, a team roper, so it was no big jump for me.

G: He's a freaking card-carrying roper! When you find out that someone has a rodeo background, well, that's a lot of good information. When you're not necessarily expecting it, even better. Steve Wynn, I find out, can ride and rope.

STEVE WYNN: There'd never been big country acts on the strip. That wasn't Las

I WAS A **JEWISH COUNTRY GUY.**
—Steve Wynn

Garth with Steve Wynn

Vegas's gig. And if country guys worked in Las Vegas, they worked the outlying bars. The country guys liked Las Vegas on a social, personal basis. Merle Haggard liked to gamble, play blackjack at the Horseshoe, but he didn't sing in Las Vegas. So, the first night we were there for the CMAs, Waylon Jennings was doing a complimentary performance, and Jimmy Dean arranged with Waylon's manager for us to go meet him. A wonderful guy. Jimmy talked about the new Gold Strike Lounge and our plans, said we wanted to open the Gold Strike Lounge with Waylon Jennings. He said, "Why not?"

G: If I could only pick one of Wynn's many gifts, it would be he knows what his customer wants.

STEVE WYNN: We struck a deal with Waylon to work for $20,000 a week. Waylon was a big star then, but he was willing to work Vegas. In that same conversation, Waylon said, "Say, hoss, you know Willie Nelson?" "No," I said. He tells me, "Well, folks down in Austin, when they die think they're going to Willie's house." I'll never forget that remark. Then he said, "I'll introduce you to him. I think he'd like to do it too." Willie Nelson joins in '74.

BOB DOYLE: Steve Wynn built a reputation for bringing the biggest acts in entertainment to Vegas. And a lot of them were country artists.

STEVE WYNN: Kenny Rogers, Nitty Gritty Dirt Band, Barbara Mandrell, Roger Miller… before Garth, yes, I had some history with country music in Las Vegas. I knew what I was going after when I went looking for Garth Brooks.

TRISHA YEARWOOD: Garth attracts interesting people. They're drawn to him, just as he's drawn to them.

G: Why Steve Wynn was looking for me was because he had built a theater for a Las Vegas performer by the name of Danny Gans. Danny was awarded the Entertainer of Las Vegas multiple times. Then Danny just didn't wake up one morning. He's mid-fifties, beautiful guy, really, really nice man, beautiful family. Steve tells me he just built this theater for a beloved entertainer, and now he's lost the entertainer. He says it's a beautiful room, that he'd like me to come out and see it. Well, I said, sure, I'll be out there to see it.

STEVE WYNN: He said he was going to go to Los Angeles and might be able to stop on the way back. I said, "Well, if you stop, I'll pick you up at the airport. We can have dinner."

G: Now, I've told Steve this story a thousand times, but I knew when I hung up that I was never, ever going to work for Steve Wynn.…But I knew Steve Wynn was going to help me tremendously with my foundation. And this was my way in.

STEVE WYNN: I went to the airport. There was a chartered Learjet there. His wife decided to stay on board. She was wearing pajamas or something. (laughs)

I WAS EXPECTING SOME REALLY BIG GUY, CHEWING ON A CIGAR. —g

TRISHA YEARWOOD: This was all about Garth's foundation. I'm not sure I was in pajamas, but I do remember that. (laughs)

STEVE WYNN: Garth came and had dinner with Andrea and me on the terrace at SW restaurant, where the Lake of Dreams is. All kinds of magic shit happens there, in the water, on the waterfalls, in the mountains. We start talking.

G: Now, Steve Wynn doesn't look like what you think a Vegas guy should. I was expecting some really big guy, you know, chewing on a cigar and real brash and loud. But this guy's quiet. He looks at me and goes, "Tell me about your family."

STEVE WYNN: Garth tells me he brought three children into the world and owes them a father, and that being a dad like his dad would be impossible for him while being a traveling and performing artist. He tells me how they and the girls' mom had been sharing custody for ten years, exchanging every day, getting to every soccer game and practice. And I'm thinking, "This is just an extraordinary story."

G: I told him what I'd tell anyone.

STEVE WYNN: Garth says, "I brought them into the world. I owe them. They don't owe me." Just like that. Andrea and I looked at each other. We began to get the shape of Mr. Brooks. Before I could get over my amazement at that answer, he said to me, "I want to ask you something. Who dreamt up all of this stuff?" And he points at the Lake of Dreams, all this magic coming out of the water. I said, "I did. With the help of a lot of other people. But the

TRISHA YEARWOOD: All Garth could talk about was this risotto he had at Steve's restaurant. Then I asked him about the foundation.

G: I said, "We never really talked about it. But I plan to when I come back…with my guitar."

TRISHA YEARWOOD: Steve Wynn is that good. (laughs)

G: After that first visit, I said, "Look, I'm going to agree that we're going to move forward talking about this deal on one condition: I want to bring my guitar and sound-check your theater, and I'm going to ask you to bring the people you love to sit in that audience. I don't care if it's ten, twenty people, but just bring the people you know and love."

STEVE WYNN IS
THAT GOOD.

—Trisha Yearwood

ideas are mine." Garth looks at me and says, "I can usually put a circle around a man, but I'm having trouble with you." I say, "In that case, we're even." That got a laugh out of him.

TRISHA YEARWOOD: When Garth arrived back at the plane, I asked him how it went.

G: I told Miss Yearwood all about Steve Wynn, the beautiful theater, the lake, the restaurant, and the killer risotto!

STEVE WYNN: He had never had risotto. (laughs)

TRISHA YEARWOOD: Garth has the ability to grab a guitar and, without planning, so spontaneously, put on a show that appears to be totally planned.

G: Doing foundation work, you'd bring your guitar. No band, just you. And when you do that kind of work, you aren't playing for your crowd, you're playing for whatever cause needs you. It's all different ages, people who don't know who Garth Brooks is, people who have heard of Garth Brooks but can't name a Garth Brooks song. So, you start to do popular songs the crowd will know, telling them how that music influenced a song of your own that you're

I WALK OUT AND EVERY SEAT IS FILLED! —g

about to play. That's what I was going to do when I sound-checked the room at the Wynn.

STEVE WYNN: I told Garth I would send the plane for him when that day comes.

G: It's a few weeks later, I'm out on my tractor, and I get the two-hour time difference mixed up. Cindy, Steve's assistant, calls and says, "Garth, the plane is there and has been waiting." I thought I had two hours. I can't even take a shower. I'm in my coveralls, grab my guitar, smelling like diesel. I get to the airport and realize he sent his personal 747. One guy, two guitars, walking up the steps of a fully staffed 747, all-white interior. I remember the flight attendant going, "You're going to have to sit down for takeoff." I said, "Ma'am, I don't even know how to sit. I smell." She says, "Just sit, you'll be fine." I got to Vegas, walked in, and explained to Steve, "I'm so sorry I look like this." Steve goes, "Don't worry about it. Come on out. I got my friends here." We walk out, and there's 1,500 people in the room, every seat filled!

STEVE WYNN: I invited all of my employees and their families. I also invite—because she

The LeFlores and the Geisslers

was working at Caesars and had the night off—Bette Midler to sit next to me. Garth Brooks comes out, empty stage, no lighting to speak of except the spotlight, and a stool with a bottle of water on it. He's got a guitar and his headset microphone. He's in his work clothes because he showed up late. Then he does this monologue about growing up, his father as a boxing champ in the Marine Corps, how he grew up with music and what he heard. He does every fucking entertainer in music from the '60s and the '70s. Paul Simon, Cat Stevens, you name it. Next, he does the '80s. Then he says, "Now, I'm going to do the '90s. And, folks, that's about me."

G: It was a little of what I'd do for my foundation work, maybe some songs I did playing Willie's Saloon in college.

STEVE WYNN: For the last part of the show, he does Garth Brooks songs. It culminates with "Friends in Low Places." The entire audience is singing everything with him, and he's laughing and enjoying it. Bette Midler leans over and says, "Are you going to book this guy? You better. My God, I've never seen anything like it." I said, "I'm real careful with this fellow. He's got a mind of his own. What he just did was his idea, not mine." She says, "Really?"

I'M REAL CAREFUL WITH THIS FELLOW.

—Steve Wynn

G: Everybody that's worked for Steve Wynn has been with him for twenty years. The mechanical guys were there that night. The people that make up the rooms were there. Steve knew every one of them. Lawyers, accountants, floor managers, everyone. I'm going to tell you, it was the coolest thing on the freaking planet. They were awesome. It was immediately a lovefest. Afterward, Steve goes, "I've got to have this show." I said, "Well, that's very sweet, but I just came to check the room, Steve. I really enjoyed the chance to play." That's when I heard for the first time what he would say again and again…

STEVE WYNN: I said, "For someone who can do what you do, it would be a crime not to do it."

TRISHA YEARWOOD: As much as he enjoyed and loved and threw himself 100 percent into being a dad, Garth was still a performer, still a writer. He couldn't hide that.

G: I told him thank you, but I just didn't see how it could work. That's when he said, "I think this deal could be easy."

STEVE WYNN: I told him the trick to this deal is we have to keep his life the way it is. We can't change anything. I said, "I know you want to take your kids to school and they're on soccer teams. And at the soccer games, you work like any other parent behind a refreshment stand. But with the time change, you could come west from Tulsa and be in Vegas when you left. And going home, it's only three hours. So, you could come on Friday after school, work Friday and Saturday, even be back home late Saturday night. Would you think about it?"

G: In the short time I had known Steve Wynn, he was really a guy I wanted to please. But as much as I wanted to say yes, how could doing this be possible?

STEVE WYNN: I said, "I tell you what, Garth. Suppose you had your own jet. You could come here. You could even go home on Friday night, be back on Saturday for the show, and you could do two shows a weekend."

G: I remember saying something silly like, "Steve, you can't afford me." We both laughed. Turns out, I was wrong. (laughs)

Wynn
In Concert
Tonight
Wynn

GARTH WAS STILL A PERFORMER.
HE COULDN'T HIDE THAT.
—Trisha Yearwood

THE SHOWS

G: Now, equipped with a plane and a plan, we announce we are coming out of retirement on the 15th of October 2009. We start in Nashville in the morning and head to Vegas for the afternoon.

STORME WARREN: I went out to Las Vegas with Bob Doyle. Steve Wynn was there, and I did a big interview with him, talking about the relationship and the deal that was made, the $100 million deal for four years. I'm like, "Holy cow." Then Garth was trying to describe the show, and none of us could envision this. Maybe he didn't even know at the time exactly what the show was going to be. But we knew we were going to see something different. And it turned out to be the coolest way ever to showcase Garth to the next generation. And a great way for old fans to reconnect with Garth in a way they never had before.

TRISHA YEARWOOD: Garth would say the Vegas show was the natural offspring of the Willie's show, what he did way back in Stillwater in college. He had all those skills from years before. I watched the show every night, and I loved it every night. People would come backstage and say how great the writing was, the script. But he didn't really write it. He just kind of did it, and it came to evolve over the several years he was there.

HOW WAS HE GOING TO PULL IT OFF?

—Storme Warren

STORME WARREN: The curiosity for all of us was how he was going to pull it off. Especially without the noise, the bells and whistles of a Garth Brooks show. He's not flying across the crowd—he's standing up there raw and vulnerable, with an acoustic guitar, telling his story.

TRISHA YEARWOOD: It was so fun. Most people, if they've seen a live show or an interview, know this serious, intimate side of Garth, but truth is, he's a big goofball. (laughs) The Vegas show gave you a chance to get to see that. You definitely laughed, you cried, you remembered the songs and why you loved them. It was so Garth.

BRYAN KENNEDY: I went out to see his Vegas show, by myself and without telling Garth. I just wanted to see what it was like for a fan to go. So, I got online, got a ticket, and stood in line to get a wristband. I did the whole thing. And I went home completely blown away. Then I let him know that I had been out there to see him. As a person who just loves entertainment, the ride of the music, the genius of playing the verse and a chorus, the humor, the emotion, well, that show had everything. When he did all that and took us on the journey from what his dad listened to, what his mom listened to, and then how that all formed into Garth, it was genius. That first

time I went, as a fan, to see what the heck he was doing—that's still the best show I've ever seen in my life. It seemed like it lasted ten minutes. I think it was two hours and twenty minutes or something.

STORME WARREN: We had missed that connection to him. So, this was an intimate way to reconnect with his fans. The timing of it was brilliant.

BOB DOYLE: Steve Wynn would sometimes liken Garth to Sinatra. I think he saw Garth as this guy who was a big presence. And in Garth's case, that meant a big enough presence that he could pull off this show without anything but his guitar and his storytelling ability. I think it was *that* that made it so special as an experience. I know so many people who would come and, at first, they'd go, "Oh, this isn't the band?" But when they walked out two and a half hours later, they couldn't believe what they'd experienced that evening. Steve Wynn is a very smart man, and I think he saw the entertainment value in that…and just went with it. Steve knew, "When there's a true entertainer, you strip it down to its raw and naked state, and it'll still hold up."

GARTH GAVE THE ROOM WHAT **FRANK SINATRA** HAD GIVEN **NEW JERSEY.**

—Steve Wynn

STEVE WYNN: All of a sudden, the Wynn had an identity because of Garth Brooks. Doing fifteen weeks, he was there a lot. All of a sudden, everybody wanted to come work. I got calls from agents. A bunch of people. All of a sudden, Garth gave the room what Frank Sinatra had given New Jersey: an entertainment personality. So, once again, that happened to me, that if you could kick off with a key guy, the right superstar, it made the venue.

STEVE WYNN
PROMISED HE WOULD
**NOT CHANGE
MY LIFE.** —g

TRISHA YEARWOOD: Vegas gave people a chance to see him in a way that I don't think anybody had. I loved it when people would come backstage, producers and actors and artists, and they'd go, "Man, how long did it take you to write this show, to craft this show?" And I'm sitting there thinking, "He's still writing it." Because I knew every night was different. What a great, great time that was.

STEVE WYNN: He became part of the family. It was his home. He thought of the hotel as just his weekend place. And everybody treated him that way at the hotel. What's better than that? For a star to be at home. Well, shit. This beloved country guy with a high-class character who took time away to be with his daughters and sang all his country music without pretense and with a sense of humor. Who else would you like to be identified with? Some fucking politician? When Garth was onstage in the Encore Theater, it was the Garth Brooks Theater.

G: So, Taylor is getting ready to be a senior in high school, playing soccer. Augie is in track and field, and Allie plays soccer and does music. Right then we had a lot to do as parents. The Wynn shows were fifteen weekends a year. I got to pick the weekends, and they were all built around the kids' schedules. Steve Wynn said he'd guarantee I would never miss a game. That's how he approached it. He promised he would not change my life. But, about that he was right and he was wrong. Because he did change my life—by making it better. Over the term of the deal, he also helped out on the foundation side. (smiles) But truth is, it was four years of knocking the rust off—without us having to change our family one bit. And to be honest, it got me thinking that maybe… just maybe, I could do this again.

UNRETIREMENT

It was 2014, the end of winter…literally and figuratively. What once was darkness, cold, and unknown, now had become safe, warm, and very nourishing. Best times, best friends, best memories. But for the first time in over a decade, the house was quiet. Maybe too quiet. Two kids in college, one left at home, but she is so busy in her senior year. So, it's just me and the love of my life with our entire future ahead of us. Ted's question from over a decade ago is ringing in my ears: "How do you not miss it?" But as much as I wondered what may still be out there, Miss Yearwood and I had become very comfortable in Oklahoma.

One day after school, Allie comes in and tells me she has decided where she would like to go to college. Since she hasn't spoken of any other college than Oklahoma State, I was not expecting what I heard. She said she wanted to go to Belmont, where Trisha went to college…in Nashville.

When I told Trisha, she was surprised as well. There's something about a last child, that "finality" of letting go. Knowing they are just "down the road" makes that letting go a bit easier. But having them "states away" makes things a little more, well, final. Trisha could see in my eyes what I was thinking.

Now it's spring, the season of new beginnings. In my dreams, I saw us moving back to Nashville, getting the band and crew back together, playing music again, and launching the "Comeback Tour." But where in the world would you launch a tour after sixteen years away from touring?

Ireland, that's where. Dublin, a guaranteed good time. So, there would be new music, new adventures, and new memories to make, as arm in arm with the love of my life we started down the "yellow brick road" to the Emerald Isle. What could possibly go wrong? (laughs)

ACKNOWLEDGMENTS

The Garth Brooks Team would like to thank the following but not limited to:
Matt Allen, Randy Bernard, Anka Brazzell, Don Cobb, Eric Conn, Jeff Crump,
the Geisslers, Charles Green, Cheryl Harris, Luellyn Latocki Hensley, Rusty Jones,
Jerry Joyner, Bryan Kennedy, Gordon Kennedy, the LeFlores, Alan Mayor Estate,
especially Theresa Mayor-Smith and Olivia M. Beaudry, Mark Miller, Craig Owens,
Pat Quigley, Allen Reynolds, Tami Rose Thompson, Jim Shaw, Nancy Seltzer,
Virginia Team, and Trisha Yearwood.

...and mostly to God, for it is through Him all things are possible.

PHOTOGRAPHY CREDITS

Butch Adams, Richard Aspinwall, Beth Bernard, Raymond Brooks, Brooks Family
Collection, David Butzler, John M. Cooper, Henry Diltz, GAPP 2002, Ltd., Lisa Geissler,
Jason Grahame, Tracy Greenwood, Russ Harrington, Brenda Hayes, Carol M. Highsmith,
Mike Jones, Bryan Kennedy, Ben Krebs, Kim LeFlore, Chris Leuzinger, Steve Lowry
Photo Archives, Alan Mayor, John McBride, Mandy McCormack, Mark Miller, Bryan Moore,
Natasha Moustache, Buck Owens Private Foundation, Bev Parker, Kevin Parry,
Jim Photoglo, Fred Reiser, Glen Rose, David Stephenson, Lynn Stewart, Rebecca Stone,
Tami Rose Thompson, Brenda Tinnen, Mark Tucker, Bobby Wood, Jenny Yates, and
Trisha Yearwood.

Image on Page 16:   Ricky Rogers - USA Today Network
Image on Page 109:   Don Putnam
Image on Page 128:   Nashville Songwriters Hall of Fame – Moments by Moser Photography
Image on Page 170:   Tony R. Phipps / WireImage

COURTESY CREDITS
George Jones appears courtesy of Bandit/BNA Records
Trisha Yearwood appears courtesy of Gwendolyn Records
Trisha Yearwood appears courtesy of MCA Records Nashville

CREDITS

Produced by:

 **MELCHER MEDIA**

Founder and CEO: Charles Melcher
Vice President and COO: Bonnie Eldon
Editorial Director: Lauren Nathan
Production Director: Susan Lynch
Executive Editor: Christopher Steighner
Senior Editor: Megan Worman
Editorial Assistant: Kevin Li